ASSEMBLY KIT

Angela Wood

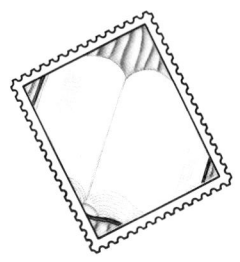

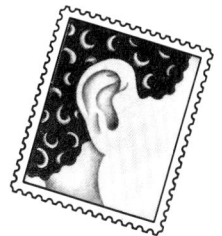

BBC Longman

For my mother
who has known me all my life
and still loves me

PUBLISHED BY BBC EDUCATIONAL PUBLISHING AND
LONGMAN GROUP UK LIMITED

BBC Educational Publishing
a division of
BBC Enterprises Limited
Woodlands
80 Wood Lane
London W12 0TT

Longman Group UK Limited,
Longman House,
Burnt Mill,
Harlow,
Essex
CM20 2JE
England, and Associated Companies
throughout the World.

First published 1991
© BBC Enterprises Limited/Longman Group UK Limited 1991

Cover & book design by Sarah Peden
Illustrated by Amanda Hall

ISBN 0 582 06783 9

Typeset by Ace Filmsetting Ltd
Text printed in Great Britain by
Bell and Bain Ltd, Glasgow
Cover printed by Richard Clay's of Bungay

All rights reserved. No part of this publication may be reproduced, stored in a retrieval system, or transmitted in any form or by any means electronic, mechanical, photocopying, recording or otherwise without the prior written permission of the Publishers or a licence permitting restricted copying issued by the Copyright Licensing Agency Ltd, 33–34 Alfred Place, London WC1E 7DP.

Contents

Assembling the Kit: how to use this book 6
You can take a horse to assembly but you can't make it worship!: some
thoughts on collective worship in schools 8

1 THE VERY START 10
Beginnings 12
Egg activities; 'Pan Gu', 'I Won't Hatch' and 'Which Came First' poems
Mix and Match Aborigine, African and Amerindian creation stories; slate-slicing anecdote; child's story about skin colours; video on newness; book box; meditation on beginnings and 'Today . . .' statement 14

2 OFF WE GO! 20
Movement, stillness and change 22
Story about three sisters searching; prayer on stillness
Mix and Match Video on travel; 'There's No Such Place As Far Away' extract; activity with wheels; Baha'i song 'Blessed is the Spot'; book box; child's reflection on Mecca; Hindu, Irish, Amerindian, African, Christian and other thoughts on movement 24

3 OFF AND ON 28
Light and darkness 30
Candle-making activity with 'Spirit of Fire' poem; African meditation on light
Mix and Match Video on light and dark; book box on Diwali; 'Kamla and Kate' extract; Chinese 'New Year Song'; lampost and lost keys story; book box on light and dark; book box on Hanukah; circle of light activity with ten quotations (including scriptures and children's sayings) 31

4 SPLASH! 36
Water 38
Activities on water; video on water; children's sayings
Mix and Match Activity on liquid, steam and ice; book box; cassette story 'Water is a Strange Thing'; story about bedouins' gift of water; Bengali song 'Come, Rain!'; Hindu story about salt in water; African Christian prayer on river 39

5 BLOWING IN THE WIND 42
Harmony with nature 44
Book box on Noah's ark; 'Rainbow' poem; Jewish story about evil and the ark; Jewish saying
Mix and Match Cassette story 'The Everglades'; video of Buddhist dance with prayer flags in wind; child's story on origin of grass and gardens; Jewish song 'Let the Heavens Shout'; book box; Indian and Amerindian meditations 46

6 THE WORLD IN OUR HANDS 50
Caring for the natural world 52
Video and book box on rain forests; child's saying
Mix and Match Buddhist story about swan and judge; book box; original song 'Growing Up' (Christian); Krishna and lapwing story; Androcles and lion story; story about Prophet Muhammad and kitten; Jewish story about planting seeds; modernised 'Twinkle, Twinkle, Little Star', Muslim sayings and Tagore quotation 53

7 FROM ME TO YOU, WITH LOVE 58
Caring for other people 60
Child's poem and video about homelessness; children's sayings about helpfulness, Cuban and

Rastafarian poem
Mix and Match Book box; child's friendship poem; original song 'A Dream of a Place' (Jewish); Jewish story of God caring through people; children's poems about love; K'Ung Fu'Tzu's questions, Jamaican poem and Christian prayer 62

8 YUMMY! I'M STARVING! 68
Feasting, fasting and famine 70
Activity on world hunger; Inuit poem; Christian prayer
Mix and Match 'Quick' harvest festival; 'Guinea Corn' poem; book box; Muslim song 'The Lord Made the Apple'; activity on *Mucky Mabel*; video on food and faith communities; cassette story 'Giving'; extract from *The Railway Children*; 'I'd like to squeeze' poem 72

9 ALL TOGETHER NOW! 78
Cooperation and community spirit 80
Video on rescue of three whales; 'Boundaries Down' poem; 'Hug O'War' poem
Mix and Match 'One Tree' poem; 'I Corinthians' extract'; book box; child's 'Recipe for Peace'; story of rejected grandmother; Muslim song 'Allah, There's Only One God'; story about parts of a tree; two poems on human unity 83

10 FAIR'S FAIR 88
Justice and equality 90
Jewish and Sikh stories about making room for people; meditation on changing the world
Mix and Match Activity on justice, truth and peace; video on death of South African miners; book box; cassette story 'Alison and the Bike'; activity on child's poem 'Stand Up For Your Rights'; original song 'What It's Worth' (Muslim); child's poem about anger; 'No Difference' poem and prayer about helplessness and help 92

11 FLYING HIGH! 98
Hope and freedom 100
Activities on freedom; *Charlotte's Web* extract; meditation on freedom
Mix and Match Video and children's poems about Berlin wall; Inuit/Amerindian story about hope; 'Bless, O Maker, Bless' song (South African, Christian); book box; activity on cellar inscription, reflections on Holocaust, Rastafarian poem, Desmond Tutu saying, Hindu quotation 102

12 ALL IN THE GAME 108
Winning and losing 110
Video on sports; child's anecdote; meditation about winning and losing
Mix and Match Activity of cooperative musical chairs; book box; 'A Fish of the World' extract; French/Creole story about jewelled eggs; original song 'Taking Sides' (Sikh); 'Exams' poem; saying of Helen Keller 111

13 YOU CAN DO IT! 118
Struggle, determination and survival 120
Jonathan Livingston Seagull extract and meditation
Mix and Match Video of squirrel on obstacle course; Jain story of four daughters-in-law with five grains of rice; 'Through the Eyes of a Dyslexic' poem; Jewish song 'You and Me'; book box; 'Jack and Jill be nimble' poem 122

14 HERE I AM 128
Sacrifice and courage 130
Bridge-crossing activity; Jewish song 'A Narrow Bridge'; meditation on bravery
Mix and Match Book box; video of girl's attempt to rescue baby from fire; *I am David* extract; Chinese story about peacock's gift; prayer about giving things up 132

15 I'LL MISS YOU 136
Losing, missing and dying 138

Activity on the death of an animal at school
Mix and Match Video and children's poems about Hillsborough; book box; Filipino song 'My Little Chick is Dead and Gone'; children's reflections on death of pets; *The Diddakoi* extract; child's poem about Grandad's death; cassette story 'Spotty Harris'; Christian prayer and Tagore poem 139

16 I'M SORRY – THAT'S OK! 146
Being hurt, saying sorry and forgiving 148

Video, children's sayings and meditation about bullying
Mix and Match Original Punjabi song 'Only One Can Talk at a Time'; book box; *The Pudding Like a Night on the Sea* extract; Christian prayer 'We Is Sorry, God' 150

17 THE REAL ME 154
Uniqueness and integrity 156

Video and child's poem about Tiananmen Square; children's sayings about standing up for your beliefs in public; statement about integrity
Mix and Match *Alice in Wonderland* extract and 'Alice' poem; Chinese puzzle on dreaming of being a butterfly; cassette story 'Chameleon'; activities on counting hairs (Christian) and heads on coins (Jewish); book box; 'Beneath the Surface' poem; *The Little Prince* extract; statement on uniqueness, Amerindian prayer and Buddhist quotation 158

18 ME AND MY BODY 164
Senses and appearances 166

'Ma and God' poem; Gujarati song 'My Body'
Mix and Match Activities on deceptive appearances; video of animals' senses; Effendi story about appearances; *The Velveteen Rabbit* extract; child's poem about hands; book box; child's meditation about sixth sense; Christian prayer about being alive 168

19 TICK! TOCK! 172
Time 174

Activity on variable times; video on relative times
Mix and Match Ecclesiastes extract; Persephone and Demeter story; *The World of Pooh* extract; book box; child's song 'Happy Times Today'; prayer about birthdays and meditation on use of time 174

20 I WONDER 180
Awe and mystery 182

Book box; child's story about dreams
Mix and Match Activity with Mobius strip; Sikh story about God being everywhere; video on Psalm 139; book box; *Anne of Green Gables* extract; *Anna's Book* extract; children's sayings about God; limerick about all-seeing God; activity on 'unheard' sounds; story about God in a cup; Special School prayer about God in everything and verse from George Herbert 184

Index of religions and cultures 190
Index of subjects 190
Acknowledgements 192

Assembling the kit
how to use this book

At some time or another, most of us have consulted a do-it-yourself manual, cut out cloth from a pattern, cooked from a recipe or constructed a household item from a flat pack claiming to be 'so easy that a child could do it'! We gain confidence from knowing that someone else has tried it before and that it is likely to work. Yet sooner or later, many of us have taken short cuts with the execution of the design, added more of this or that to the dish, altered the line of the garment or at least painted the object in the colour of our choice! The circumstances in which we are working, our previous experience and our individualism lead us to depart from structure and formal advice.

The twin needs for security and flexibility in collective worship lie at the heart of *Assembly Kit*. Each of the twenty chapters contains a 'worked example' which has been used in Primary schools and which could be conducted as it stands. Taken as a whole, these also serve as models and offer twenty different styles of assembly employing a range of items and varied lines of development. The second part of each chapter, headed 'Mix and Match', contains material to substitute for some of the pieces in the 'worked example', to compose other assemblies on the same theme or to combine with favourite pieces already in the teacher's repertoire. The permutations are almost infinite!

In opening up for children an exploration of what it means to be a human being and a reflection on their own inner world, the material is selected not only from explicit religious phenomena but also from apparently 'ordinary' experiences which are yet vibrant with meaning and in which beliefs and values may be implicit. Examples are drawn from several world faiths and many cultures, for the life of the spirit knows no bounds.

Some items explore aspirations and achievements; some express joy, humour, wonder and celebration; some cover political events which have become keystones in modern life, even for young children; and some deal with tragedy and suffering in the firm conviction that respect for children involves giving them an opportunity to come to terms with life's difficulties. It is hoped that nothing patronises children, but is rather offered in the belief that they are able to appreciate far more than they can ever articulate.

There are several typefaces: large print applies to those poems, sayings, stories and extracts which are suitable for children, with some preparation, to read aloud. The text in bold print addresses the pupils: it could be used verbatim as an introduction or simply as a source of ideas to be adapted by teachers wishing to make their own presentation.

The detailed table of contents has two purposes. It not only shows at a glance what appears under each theme but can also locate a particular element which teachers have drawn from before and want to employ again in another context. The index of religions and cultures and the index of subjects on pages 190/191 are intended to help teachers bring together material for a special focus on a particular group of people or on a specific topic.

Each chapter opens with a large photograph which could be shared with a single class or a small group able to see it at close range and is particularly accessible to young children. It is also effective to open the book at the picture, prop it up on a stand and display it on the hall table for all to see as they pass.

In the chapters, there are margin headings and stamps beside each element which identify its medium or mode of delivery:

The video: this refers to one of the clips in the accompanying video cassette, also titled *Assembly Kit*, and each lasts about three minutes. This is best seen by a relatively small group of children but it is feasible to show it to quite a large gathering as it is succinct and short enough for some children to stand and watch.

Video is a medium not yet exploited for collective worship yet there are many human experiences which are difficult to communicate to children through the spoken word alone; and the unique contribution of this visual form is its ability to convey texture and capture atmosphere. Indeed, worship aspires to a condition that is 'beyond words'.

The notes on each clip are intended to give enough information to be able to show it with confidence. Ideally, the teachers involved should see the video beforehand so as to use it most effectively and to be aware of issues and situations which touch their pupils. But schools are busy places and the demands on teachers are so great that adequate time for preparation is not always available. The notes indicate which sequences would actually be inadvisable to show without previewing. These have a 'Handle With Care' label.

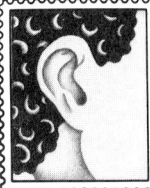
The cassette: an accompanying tape of six stories and plays, also entitled *Assembly Kit*, links with the themes in which they are described but could be listened to in other contexts.

The song: all of these are new to assembly books. Some are traditional but unpublished and have been transcribed specially; others are original compositions. The vocal line is given as well as some suggestions for musical setting which could involve piano, recorder, guitar or simple percussion.

Many of the songs appear in dual language, with an English version which fits the melody as well as the transliterated lyric. Unless there are in the school children or staff who speak the language in question, it may be wise to begin by learning the English words and then progress to the source language when all are confident with the music. While this is less authentic, it may be more realistic and less likely to inhibit any appreciation of the song at all.

Book box: far from being an exhaustive list, this is a 'starter kit', mostly comprising picture books and other literature that will appeal to the younger age range. In most chapters, the books relate to the theme in an overall sense, but in some there is also a book box on a specific aspect.

To read out and *To read out or act*: there is great diversity of source and form, including children's writing, extracts from novels (mainly for the top of the Primary age range), poems, anecdotes, traditional stories retold and quotations from scripture.

Most can be presented by accomplished readers and those that are particularly fitting are printed in large type: unless the child has great stamina, the extracts from novels are too long for one and an appropriate point to change readers is marked in the following way: ●, ▲ and ■. Role play, mime and other forms of drama are suggested and, although these invariably involve both preparation and stage fright, they do much to bring the narratives to life and to engage performers and viewers with the ideas they contain.

Activities: some are simple discussion points or puzzles but most are suggestions for rituals and spiritual exercises which encourage children, through movement and an appreciation of their senses, to experience and inwardly explore an aspect of the theme. They are intended to create an awareness that collective worship is an 'act'.

Closing thoughts: as well as traditional prayers, there are poems, quotations from scripture, sayings and specially created meditations which are intended to draw some threads together and to permit personal reflection in silence and stillness. As the creation of an atmosphere conducive to this innerness is vital, these closing thoughts are best presented by adults.

In schools which have a religious foundation, some of the more open-ended passages can be set in the context of a prayer, either by beginning with an address to God and ending with 'Amen' or by offering the meaning of the words to God, perhaps like this: 'This poem really makes me feel how much I love you . . .' or 'Please help me to be more . . . like the person who said . . .'

Some closing thoughts are formal prayers addressing the Almighty and may be compromising for some individuals or inappropriate in their settings: it is theoretically possible to adjust the wording yet this seems dishonest and offensive. Rather than avoid using such pieces, it might be worth considering a form of words such as this:

'Let's all be quiet together. If you like, you can close your eyes . . . I am going to read something which is very special to . . . Think about what it might mean for them . . . for you . . . or all of us.'

You can take a horse to assembly but you can't make it worship!

Amid the overwhelming demands for innovation and implementation that teachers face, collective worship remains one of the greatest educational challenges of the day . . . not least because school worship is quite different from worship within a home or faith community, where there is probably unanimity of beliefs or an accepted philosophy of life. Schools which see themselves as a community strive for consistent values and coherent patterns of behaviour; yet they are essentially pluralist places for their members bring varied ways of life and views of life. Indeed, a school may represent all faiths and none.

The challenge, then, is to create an occasion which . . .

neither imposes nor compromises belief or unbelief, but rather recognises the integrity and dignity of all members of the school community; and

stimulates and cultivates the experience of reflecting inwardly, sharing outwardly and living upwardly.

What is worship?

Collective worship is part of the whole curriculum which is intended to promote the 'spiritual, moral, cultural, mental and physical development of pupils and of society' and prepare pupils 'for the opportunities, responsibilities and experiences of adult life' (1988). The DES also refers to the 'quality and relevance . . . of religious worship in the curriculum' and to its 'special place in the school curriculum' (3/89)

Yet neither the ERA nor the DES defines worship: because either its meaning is too obvious to be stated or, conversely, the enormous divergence of views makes consensus impossible! A tightly worded definition would violate worship's elusive and mystical qualities, yet schools will need to negotiate some sense of its meaning and purpose, however tenuous. County schools would do well to consult LEA guidelines, and Voluntary schools those of their Diocese or Trust.

Dictionaries generally offer two definitions of worship, one 'narrow' – reverence for a divine being or supernatural power; and one 'broad' – respect for an object of esteem. Too 'narrow' an approach at school is unlikely to take account of the family backgrounds, ages and aptitudes of the pupils as the law requires; while the 'broad' approach risks missing the special role of worship in a school where *much* is worthy.

Assembly Kit follows a middle way and sees worship as . . .

an awareness of being in the presence of something or someone greater than oneself, that is both beyond and within all life; reaching out to and being enriched by that ultimate reality.

This book meets a variety of school situations: much of its content is 'broadly Christian' but it recognises that many teachers feel relatively well served with Christian resources and most acutely need a wide range of other material.

The spirit and the child

The spiritual development of pupils – the first educational aim stated in the ERA 1988 – and what have come to be called 'spirituality across the curriculum' and children's 'spiritual entitlement' lie at the heart of the quality of worship that children can be offered. These 'human capacities' (delineated by Maurice Lynch) evoke rather than define the paradox of human spirituality and point to a reality which is deep and full:

- a sense of awe, wonder and mystery
- a sense of transience and constant change
- a sense of pattern, order and purpose
- an awareness of, and relationship with, the natural world
- an awareness of, and relationship with, others as feeling, thinking persons
- an awareness of community – its demands, values and rituals
- an awareness of achievement, celebration and joy
- an awareness of loss, sadness and suffering
- an awareness that life involves choices – between good and bad, right and wrong, being outgoing and being selfish

A time and a place

The special nature of school worship calls for a special approach and a first step might be coining a special name: 'daily act of collective worship' is laughably clumsy and incomprehensible to Primary pupils; 'assembly' is widespread yet refers to many occasions on which 'two or three are gathered together' (or, indeed, two or three classes or two or three hundred pupils!) and is meaningless if applied to worship in an individual classroom since the children are assembled there anyway! Perhaps the children could devise a name and so understand it better: some have come up with 'special time', 'thinking space' and 'together moment'.

The setting should be conducive to a respectful and reflective atmosphere. For the hall, children might create a mural or table display in a focal point – put up specially for the occasion to symbolise both involvement and transformation. For their own classroom, they might make a tablecloth, or a band to encircle their space, or a patchwork sheet on which to sit.

Protecting that time is vital, too, especially given the flexibility that is now possible: the anxiety that someone might pop in at any moment with the dinner-money tin or a message for the teacher – and ruin the whole thing! – is both disturbing and inhibiting. The children could solve this by designing a 'Please do not disturb us now. We're having our . . .' sign to hang on the door or, in an open classroom, display on a stand beside the area: *everyone* should respect it.

There is silence and there is silence . . .

Most know the difference between having to be quiet because they have been naughty – or no one can stand the noise any longer! – and being invited to respond privately to something they have experienced. Duration may depend as much on the weather as the climate of the school and varies according to the pupils' age and aptitudes. It is not wise to prolong the silence to the point where it becomes negative but rather develop the discipline gradually: it has been known for six year olds to be quiet and still for as long as ten minutes. Paradoxically, listening can promote quiet reflection and create a positive mood, and children are capable of more silence than is generally audible!

These publications include explanations and discussions of the legal aspects of collective worship:
British Council of Churches, *Worship in Education*, 1989, ISBN 0 85169 205 2.
Free Church Federal Council, *Collective Worship in County Schools: a Guide to Principles and Practice*, 1990 (27 Tavistock Square, London WC1H 9HH).
Bill Gent, *School Worship: Perspectives, Principles and Practice*, Christian Education Movement, 1989, ISBN 1 85100 006 2 (esp pp. 6–12 which identify six key principles).
John M. Hull, *The Act Unpacked*, Christian Education Movement, 1989, ISBN 1 85100 060 7.
Standing Conference on Interfaith Dialogue in Education, *The Education Reform Act 1988: a Brief Guide to Religious Education and Worship*, 1989 (88 Brondesbury Villas, London NW6 6AD).
Recorded instrumental music which is easy to obtain and has been successfully used with Primary children includes:
'Instrumental Greats' (Polygram CBS, BMG; STAC 2341), 'Instrumental Magic' (K-TEL International; OCE 2438) and 'Themes for Dreams' (K-TEL International; OCE 2077).

1 The very start

For children, many things happen for the first time. They explode with excitement at the creation of something new and the supreme experience is the birth of a baby, which betokens the beginning of the universe. In many creation stories, life emerged from a primordial cell – quite often depicted as an egg.

beginnings

An activity

One or more of these very simple egg 'tricks' can serve to invite children to explore in a quite concrete way the otherwise very abstract concepts of creation and newness:

Cover the picture of a bird hatching from an egg with a sheet of paper at least the same size. Gradually, pull the cover from the picture, revealing the image slowly. Stop every now and then to ask the children what they think it is! Expose the whole image whether they guessed it right or not!

Try to obtain a wooden (or plastic or ceramic) egg – especially the kind which has a model of a baby bird inside – or make one up from Easter egg 'shells'. If it is small enough, cup it in your hands and ask the children to speculate what you have there and to reflect on what it might feel like to be a baby bird inside an egg. They may do this privately or share their thoughts with a friend or even the whole gathering.

Have ready a raw and a hard-boiled egg. Without the children seeing, lay a soft cloth on the table, place the *raw* egg in the middle and fold the cloth back over the egg so that the opening is on the side of the table nearest the children. The bump should be apparent. You might like to fool the children that there is a live animal inside (by saying things like, 'Ssh! Don't frighten the poor little thing!' or 'Let's lift up the cloth a bit to give it some air!'). You may prefer to play it straight. One approach is to say that you will quickly lift the cloth and then let it down again in a flash so they had better keep their eyes open! When they have guessed that it is an egg, crack it carefully into a glass bowl. Allow the children to look at the yolk and the albumen, the tenuous way they are joined and any markings on the yolk. Then ask for a volunteer to crack the other (that is, hard-boiled!) egg! Choose a child who can take a joke! Discuss the difference between the two eggs. Which one seems newer or more alive?

Many creation stories involve an egg as the primordial cell of life; certainly children recognise it as elemental and it is an archetypal image of origins, growth and newness.

To read out or act

In a creation story from China, Pan Gu is the original being who began in an egg and from whom the entire universe is derived and therefore interconnected.

Stephen Clark wrote 'Pan Gu' originally as a music-drama piece for a Primary class. He says: 'There are many ways of dramatising this and the song stands on its own if drama does not seem appropriate.'

Pan Gu

No birds, no bees,
No sun, no breeze,
No hills, no trees,
No light, no seas.

Pan Gu slept for a long, long time
In an egg, dreaming of the light.
Pan Gu waited as the years went by
In his egg: all he knew was night.
Pan Gu!
What are you waiting for?
Pan Gu!
It's time to break the door
And let the world take flight.

Pan Gu woke from his deep, deep sleep
In his egg and couldn't see the light.
Pan Gu shouted out but no one heard
In his egg, so he began to fight.
Pan Gu!
It's time to break the shell!
Pan Gu!
It's time to leave your cell
And let the world take flight!

Pan Gu pushed with all his heart!
Pan Gu pushed the world apart!

Pan Gu stopped when his job was done
And the land was miles from the sky.
Pan Gu knew he could do no more
Then he fell, knowing he would die.
Pan Gu!
Now you have done your task.
Pan Gu!
What more could anyone ask?
It's time to say goodbye!

Pan Gu's breath gave us wind and clouds
And his blood flowed into the seas.
Pan Gu died but he gave us life
And his hair grew into the trees.
Pan Gu!
He died for everyone.
Pan Gu!
His eyes became the sun
That shines upon the breeze.

Stars and gold
And hills and streams
Started with old
Pan Gu's dreams.

(Originally, some children acted out the story while the others sang and played the song. The drama consisted of a child sitting on the floor during the first verse, surrounded by six others with their arms joined over her/his head to represent the egg. During the second verse, the child in the middle pushed against the others until he/she broke free, leaving the 'pieces of egg' scattered on the floor. In the third verse, the child slowly melted to the ground and finally, during the fourth verse, the children who were pieces of egg became trees, mountains, forests, rivers, the sun and the moon.)

Closing thoughts

I Won't Hatch!

'Oh, I am a chickie who lives in an egg,
But I will not hatch, I will not hatch.
The hens they all cackle, the roosters all beg,
But I will not hatch, I will not hatch.
For I hear all the talk of pollution and war
As the people all shout and the airplanes roar,
So I'm staying in here where it's safe and it's warm,
And I WILL NOT HATCH!'

(Shel Silverstein, *Where the Sidewalk Ends*, Harper and Row, 1974, 006 025667 2, p. 127.)

Which Came First?

'Which came first,
The chicken or the egg?
Some say the chicken,
Some say the egg.

If you didn't have an egg
to hatch from the very start
how could you have had a chicken?
But then again, without a chicken
you wouldn't have had an egg.

The argument goes on and on.

But one bright little egg
with a mysterious nod
says the very first egg
was laid by God

and mislaid by the Devil.

So whether the very first chicken
was hatched in heaven or hell

no one can tell.'

(John Agard, *Laughter is an Egg*, Viking, 1990, 0 670 82730 4, p. 47.)

Mix and match

An activity

The Aborigines are one of the oldest peoples in the world and have lived in the place that Westerners call 'Australia' for over forty thousand years. They dwell in harmony with the land and believe that all creatures have ancestors who have existed deep within it since the dawn of creation, the Dreamtime.

A potent experience of this story involves varying numbers of children standing up (or raising their hands, as agreed) at the mention of certain words. In this way, key concepts are introduced and their relative significance is communicated through the size of the bodily response! The cast of 'standers' might look something like this:

earth: everyone

The Great Builder: no one (but pause, even so)

men: a man and a boy

women: a woman and a girl

animals: a random group (e.g. those wearing white socks)

birds: a random group (e.g. those wearing black shoes)

Dreamtime: a random group (e.g. those with long hair)

ancestors: another random group (e.g. those with short hair)

To read out

The asterisks (*) serve as reminders that a key word has just appeared and that a moment's pause should be given to allow those concerned to stand and sit down again.

Long ago, there was only the earth*, completely flat, dry and bare – dead, it seemed. No animals* ran back and forth and no birds* flew up above.

Deep in the earth* lived the ancestors* of the Dreamtime* and the Great Builder* brought them up, one by one. Some of them looked like men* and women*; some of them looked like animals* or birds*; yet others could change their shape into anything so that it was impossible to tell what they really were.

The ancestors* of the Dreamtime* wandered over the earth* and many exciting things happened: sometimes they bumped into other ancestors* and sometimes it was friendly and sometimes it was not so friendly. Sometimes there were even arguments and fights between the ancestors* or wars with the animals*. But whatever happened changed the earth* forever, for men* and women*, animals* and birds* – and the ancestors* of the Dreamtime*.

To read out or act

An African creation story as retold by a group of nine-year-olds at Salusbury Junior School.

The vomiting idea is difficult for some children to accept or take seriously: unpleasant connotations are lessened if the children merely perceive that the creatures 'came out of' Mbombo. Take a very large cardboard carton and remove the flaps on both the small ends. Around one end, stick on lips and teeth cut from red and white card or paper. Face this end of the carton towards the assembled gathering to evoke a huge open mouth. Ask children to play the part of the created beings and to suggest the role by a simple costume or mask, or by carrying an object which symbolises that being, for example, a banana for a monkey. These actors line up at the back door of the mouth, so to speak, and, as the story unfolds, they crawl through the carton and emerge from the open mouth.

14

In the beginning there was nothing but darkness and water ruled over by Mbombo. One day Mbombo felt terrible pains in his stomach and he vomited up the sun, moon and the stars. Now there was light everywhere and the fierce rays of the sun made the water turn to steam and rise up as clouds.

Mbombo vomited again and this time trees came out of his mouth, followed by animals, the first woman, the leopard, the eagle, the falling star, the anvil, the monkey, the first man, the razor, medicine and lightning.

Lightning was the only trouble-maker and had such a fierce temper and caused so much trouble that Mbombo chased it into the sky where it lives today.

To read out

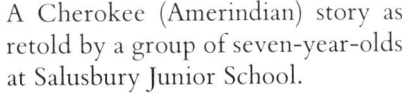

A Cherokee (Amerindian) story as retold by a group of seven-year-olds at Salusbury Junior School.

In the beginning, there was only water. Animals were above the water in a land called Gulun'lati. They were happy enough but it was very crowded and they wanted more room. They wondered what was below the water. At last the little water beetle offered to go and see if it could find out. It darted over the surface but could find no firm place to rest. Then it dived to the bottom of the water and came up with some soft mud which began to grow and spread until it became the island which we call the Earth. It was afterwards fastened to the sky with four cords but no one remembered who did this. ●

At first the earth was very soft and wet. The animals wanted to get down and sent out different birds to see if it was dry. But the birds ▶

came back because there was no dry place for them to perch on. At last it seemed to be time, so they sent the great buzzard from Gulun'lati and told him to go and make the earth ready for them.

When he reached the Cherokee country, he was exhausted. His wings began to sag and strike the ground as he flew. Wherever they struck the ground there became a valley and where the wings turned up there became a mountain. The Cherokee country remains full of mountains even today.

It was still dark when the animals decided it was dry enough to come down, so they got the sun and set it to go in a track every day across the earth from east to west.

. . . .

To read out

Try to have a piece of slate to hold up for the children to see.

In northern Wales, where there are quite a lot of mountains, for hundreds of years miners have been going deep into the mountains and bringing up huge slabs of grey slate. They used to load it onto hand-carts and pull them out but now they have small trains. When the slabs of slate are brought up, someone slices them with a special cleaver into thin, even slates. Then they can be used for roof tiles.

A little girl visited a slate mine and was fascinated to see how hard the skilled craftsman concentrated on slicing the slate into wafer-thin slivers, one after the other, every one even and straight. She said to him, 'Is that boring . . . just cutting one slice after another of dull grey slate?'

He put down his cleaver and looked at her. 'Boring? Not at all! First of all, no two slices of slate are the same: some are dark, some are light; some are shiny, some are matt; some are smooth, some are rough. And then there's something very special . . . you see these slabs of slate? They've been in the ground for millions of years and when I cut a slice of slate and it topples on its side, it's like a face looking up at me. And I know I'm the very first person in all the world to see it! That's why my work is exciting, not boring!'

To read out or act

The girl who wrote this story was particularly concerned to understand ethnic differences. Visualising the central sequence – involving the four colours – will bring it to life and can be effected by four children acting as the discoverers of the body. Smearing themselves in paint would be messy and likely to encourage frivolity; but draping themselves in lengths of cloth in the appropriate colours and running into four different directions of the hall or classroom would make the point simply.

Why do people have different coloured skins and languages?

A long time ago, the whole world lived together in a very large mass of land. They all looked exactly alike and behaved in the same way. Often they liked the same things and so they fought over lots of small silly things.

One day two young men were fighting over a young girl. Both wanted to marry her. The girl was very frightened. She did not want sorrow and hatred in the world. She wanted joy and laughter for everyone. She went to sleep, crying over her problem. That night she went to the temple and prayed for help over her troubles. Her mind was very mixed and she was in utter confusion. She walked into a fish-market, picked up a knife and ran in the direction of the woods. On her way, she took with her a pot of yellow mustard, a piece of coal, brown gravy colouring and white chalk. She ran as far as her feet would carry her and then she plunged the knife into her chest. She died in a pool of blood, the reddest ever seen. ●

The next day everyone was looking for the girl and a young girl went into the woods, hoping to find her friend. She saw her in a pool of blood and realised that she had killed herself. She looked around her and saw the mustard, coal, gravy browning and chalk and the knife on the floor beside the body. She realised that this must be a present for the gods to allow her into the next world. She then began to think ahead: people might accuse *her* of killing her friend! She had an idea: she smeared her face and body with the yellow mustard and ran into a different part of the forest. A man came that way into the forest, noticed the body and realised that if they found him near the body, they'd think he'd killed the girl. So he smeared his face and body with the black coal as a disguise. Then he ran away into a different part of the forest. ▶

Another girl came, too; she smeared her face and body with the gravy browning and ran away. Then a young man came, saw what fate held in store, covered his face and body with the chalk and ran as fast as he could to a different part of the forest. ▲

The chieftain was getting worried and decided to look for the people who were missing. He found the dead body and carried it back to the village. The villagers and the rest of the world were shocked, appalled and very angry. Later that night, the gods sent a terrible rain and hurricane storm which flooded the world. It caused all the streams, rivers and seas to overflow and kill most of the people. Pieces of land floated around, away from one other. The seas were very rough and took days to get calm again.

The surviving people climbed on to the land and started to live different lives. They met the people of different coloured skins and their numbers multiplied. Their beliefs and rituals changed as the years went on, so did their languages. This is how we have black skinned peoples, brown, yellow and white.

(Jacqueline Richards, age 11)

The video

Clip number 1 on the accompanying video cassette is a montage of several experiences of newness or beginning, taken from human life and the natural world. Time lapse is used to speed up plant processes!

If time and technology permit, it is helpful for the children to see the whole clip straight through and be given a few moments to air their overall impressions. Then, with the aid of the counter on the video recorder, rewind to the beginning of the clip and show each sequence in turn, using the pause facility. It might be useful to ask the children, 'What's new here?' or 'What is beginning?' In the sequences of plants and seeds, they might also be invited to explore what part, if any, human beings are playing in the process of new life. You might then like to play the whole sequence right through again.

Everything we know through our senses began at some time. Perhaps it was suddenly quite new or perhaps it took a long time. You'll see plants growing and people changing: when you see them, ask yourself, 'What's new? What's beginning?'

You'll see someone sowing seeds and the grass growing; you can hear birds singing.

You may wonder why there is a board outside a house saying 'Sold' and flapping in the wind . . . You'll soon find out . . .

Two toddlers, one living in Kenya and one in England, are learning to walk. Which one do we see making it first? From the look on her face, how does she feel?

Flowers are opening . . . it doesn't happen so quickly but the camera was speeded up!

A man and a woman are locking up a house and driving away in a van. Then they unload some of their things into a new home.

A seed pod is shaking in the wind and the seeds are falling. What will happen next?

Book box

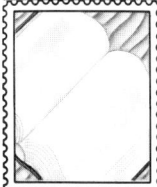

Michael Foreman, *Ben's Baby*, Beaver Books, 1989, 0 09 958700 9. Ben wanted a baby for his next birthday present and seems to have planted the seed of the idea in his parents' mind.

Janet and Allan Ahlberg, *Bye Bye Baby*, Heinemann, 1989, 0 434 92426 8. Subtitled 'a sad story with a happy ending', this story appears to trace child development in reverse!

Francis Mosley, *The Dinosaur Eggs*, Piper Books, 1989, 0 330 30639 1. A childless couple find three unusual eggs which hatch when they get them home.

Eric Carle, *The Tiny Seed*, Picture Knight, 1987, 0 340 42836 8. The autumn wind blows a tiny sunflower seed into the sky and it continues to be buffeted about in the world and encounters many threats to its existence.

Margaret Greaves, 'Once There Were No Pandas' (China), pp. 9–14; Rene Buckley, 'Wambu the Duck' (Australia), pp. 89–96; in The Federation of Children's Book Groups, *Stories Round the World*, Hodder and Stoughton, 1990, 0 340 51270 9. Two creation stories in an anthology of myths, legends and fairy tales.

Martin Palmer and Esther Bisset, *Worlds of Difference*, Blackie/World Wildlife Fund, 1985, 0 216 91666 6. A range of creation stories with specifically religious perspectives.

Closing thoughts

This is best heard with eyes closed. After each 'think of' allow the children time to bring such an image to mind and savour it. The last verse refers to some adult experiences and substitutions might be made instead, such as, 'paddling in the sea', 'catching snowflakes' and 'feeding a tiny kitten'.

In the beginning, God made the world.
Let us give thanks for all that God has made.

Think of a time when you saw that the world is
   beautiful . . .
Think of a sunset over the hills,
   or sunrise over a sleeping city.
Think of a running river,
   or stars shining on a dark sea.

Think of light flashing on a puddle,
   or of geraniums growing in a window-box.

Think of a time when you saw that the world is
   beautiful
   – and give thanks.

Think of a time when you found pleasure in your
   body . . .
Think of walking in the wind, or digging a garden.
Think of dancing till dawn, or climbing a
   mountain.
Think of giving birth to a child,
   or of holding someone you love.
Think of a time when you found pleasure in your
   body
   – and give thanks.

(The Iona Community, *Iona Community Worship Book*, Wild Goose Publications, 1988.)

Today is the first day of the rest of my life.

This could be projected overhead or displayed on a banner throughout all the assemblies on the theme of newness. If not, it can be easily memorised and recited collectively – both to draw together ideas about what has been created and also to suggest that people can be actively involved in the process of creation through what they make of their own lives.

2

Off we go!

Children love toy vehicles and playing holiday games, and seem to be intrigued by all kinds of journeys, including outings and pilgrimages. Implicit in this is the idea of travel in the mind, of life as a pilgrimage. Sometimes there is a need to resist movement and change, to permit stillness and quiet.

movement, stillness and change

To read out or act

The importance of stillness and quiet is exemplified in this adaptation of a parable-in-action, which has been used in women's groups in the Philippines for training in self-awareness and social change. It is Chinese in origin, possibly of Buddhist tradition, and it lends itself to dramatisation or mime by three girls and the only props needed are two cushions and a large glass bowl filled with muddy water. In a large gathering, not all the children will be able to see the muddy water stirred and settle and that may need to be repeated in their classes.

Once there were three sisters who were very different but each of them wanted to find out for herself what life was all about and wanted to do something good.

The eldest said, 'I am going to help look after the sick. I will bring them health and happiness.'

The middle sister said, 'I am going to sort out people's arguments. I will bring them peace and friendship.'

The youngest of the three said, 'I am staying here.'

The older two scoffed at her, 'Why aren't *you* going to go anywhere or do anything? You lazy thing!'

I never said I wouldn't *do* anything,' she replied. 'I just said that I am staying here.'

Without really thinking about what she meant, the two of them said goodbye to her and to each other, and set off on their journeys.

After a year, they came back, tired and sad. The eldest one sighed, 'I can't do it! There are so many people and they are all so ill! What chance do I have?'

The second one added, 'The same thing happened to me! It's no good trying to stop all the fights and rows by myself! It really gets me down!'

Their younger sister patted two cushions on the grass and beckoned them to sit down. Then she drew from the river a glass bowl of muddy water and set it on the ground in front of them. 'What can you see in there?' she enquired of them.

They peered in. 'Nothing!' they answered.

'Now, wait! Let it stand and settle . . .' The water became still, the mud started to sink to the bottom of the bowl and the top began to clear. 'Ooh! Look!' they said. 'That's us!' as they caught their own reflection in the water.

'You see,' the youngest one explained, 'when the water is all stirred up, it's muddy and only when it's still is it clear. It's like that with us: we have to be still to be clear about ourselves, to see what we're really like. When we know who we are and where we come from, then we can choose what to do.'

. . . .

Closing thought

Dear God,

We live in such a busy, noisy world. We need times in our life when all we can hear is our own breathing or a bird singing in the trees.

Thank you for people that we don't always need to say something to.

Thank you for this moment to stop and be still, to think, to wait, to pray and just to be who we are.

Mix and match

The video

Several modes of transport appear in clip number 2 on the accompanying video cassette. Some are fast and some slow; some are modern, some traditional and some undergoing revival; some are for the purpose of getting 'from A to B' and some for the sheer excitement of the journey itself. Seeing them together is intended to help the children appreciate that travel is diverse and all special journeys evoke quite powerful emotions and aspirations.

This clip will work best if the children have a chance to see each sequence separately as well as straight through (see notes on clip number 1 on page 18).

You'll see some ways in which people travel. In each one, ask yourself what it might feel like to travel that way. Which do you think is most comfortable? Which is most exciting? How would you like to travel to school each day? How would you like to travel to a special place you had never visited before?

A hot-air balloon is floating across the sky . . . the music you hear is played on an Indian instrument called a sitar.

Racing cars are speeding round the track. It's very dangerous so why do you think some people enjoy this sport so much?

A high-speed train is crossing a bridge over some water. Then it seems that you're actually driving the train! Look out for children playing on the beach as the train passes and then a criss-cross pattern as it whizzes past the railings.

A man is mounting a camel in the desert: watch how the camel gets up! Does it seem to mind?

A girl is sliding down a water chute, getting faster all the time. It suddenly stops and goes blank – what has happened?

A man and a boy get into a roller coaster. It goes up and down, round and round. What feeling can you see on their faces?

To read out or act

Simple paraphrasing and light dramatisation can make the quite sophisticated concepts of this passage accessible to most children.

'I began my journey in the heart of the hummingbird . . . He was friendly as ever, yet when I told him that little Rae was growing up and that I was going to her birthday party with a present, he was puzzled. We flew for a long while in silence and at last he said, "I understand very little of what you say, but least of all do I understand that you are *going* to the party."

"Of course I am going to the party," I said. "What is so hard to understand about that?" He was quiet . . . then he said, "Can miles truly separate us from friends? If you want to be with Rae, aren't you already there?"'

(Richard Bach, *There's No Such Place As Far Away*, Delacorte Press, 1979, 0 440 08780 5, pp. 6–10.)

An activity

This is a simple demonstration of the paradox of movement and stillness. You will need a globe that rotates about its axis and a wheel that spins – an upturned bicycle will do!

There is something funny and wonderful about moving circles. Stay completely still: does the ground feel as if it is moving? It doesn't, does it? But look – we're on the world like this globe, it's round and it's spinning fast . . .

Now let's spin this bicycle wheel as fast as we can . . . Whee! Does it look as if it's all moving – the hub, the rim, the spokes and everything? There is something very mysterious about this: do you know that right in the middle, in the very centre of the wheel, it is absolutely still?

(Children can try the wheel exercise for themselves with toy vehicles.)

The song

Blessed Is The Spot

This Baha'i song, based on the writings of Baha'u'llah, complements the video clip perfectly and is particularly effective if each phrase referring to a place (e.g. 'and the mountain') is sung by a different voice. This allows many children to take part – yet not to have a hefty piece to learn! – and to sing in a suitable pitch. Children's art depicting the various 'types' of places could be displayed on walls or in 'show-and-tell' style.

A children's book of the same title and illustrated with a global perspective by Anna Stevenson is published by The National Spiritual Assembly of the Baha'is (1958; 4th printing 1987).

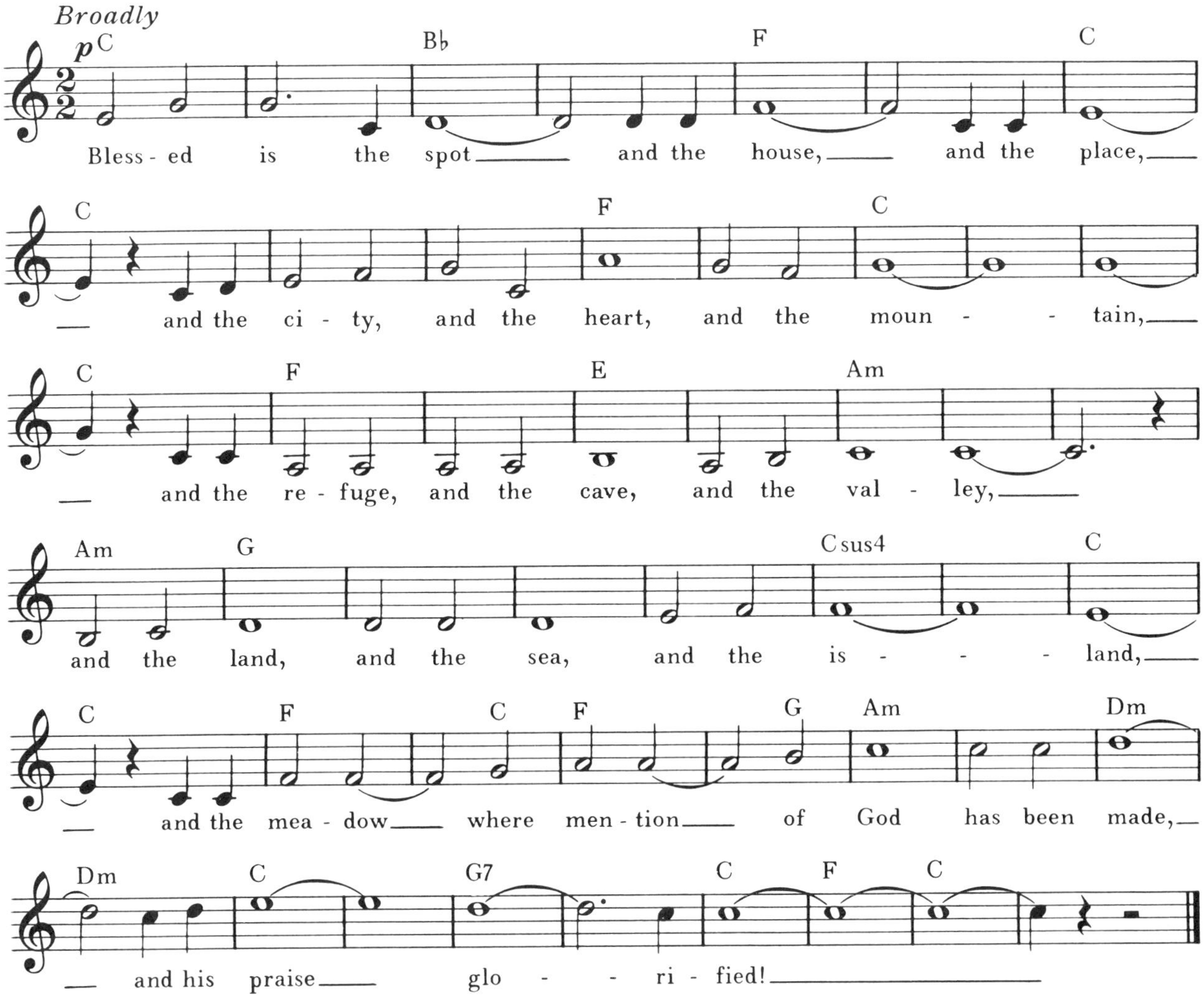

Book box

John Burningham, *Mr Gumpy's Outing*, Picture Puffin, 1985, 0 14 050254 8. Everyone goes along for a ride in a boat!

Quentin Blake, *Patrick*, Picture Puffin, 1979, 0 14 050021 9. As Patrick goes along, interesting things happen to people who hear him play his violin with special powers.

Robert Kraus, *Where Are You Going, Little Mouse?*, Macmillan, 1988, 0 333 46415 X. A book to delight very young children (and adults!) on the profound theme that our journeys of exploration lead us to find that what we seek has always been at home.

Jez Alborough, *The Grass is Greener*, A. and C. Black, 1986, 0 7136 2809 X. A humorous variation on the old chestnut.

Angela Wood, 'Cup Final' in *Faith Stories for Today*, BBC/Longman, 1990, 0 582 05946, pp. 58–63. An imaginative and modernised treatment of the Holy Grail legends.

Jill Paton Walsh, *Babylon*, Andre Deutsch, 1982, 0 233 97362 1. A warming story of a black girl's quest for identity and belonging. It will help to read Psalm 137:1–6 and sing or listen to any one of the musical settings which have made it famous.

Oliver Hunkin (ill.), *The Dangerous Journey* after John Bunyan, *Pilgrim's Progress*, Marshall Morgan and Scott/Channel 4, 1985, 0 551 012188. A richly illustrated large format book of the classic allegory of a Christian's journey through life.

Angela Wood, 'Inside Out' in *Faith Stories for Today*, BBC/Longman, 1990, 0 582 05946 1. An account of a pilgrimage to Mecca and the effects perceived by some mice!

To read out

Mecca is the heart of the Islamic world and every Muslim hopes to visit it as a pilgrim at least once in their lifetime. This is written by Saima Chaudry, a Muslim teenage girl, who said, 'This is an account of a visit to Mecca.' Her Sikh friend, Ravinder Dhinosa, helped her put her feelings into words.

In the name of Allah, most gracious, most merciful:

It was the most beautiful thing I saw. As I began praying, my tears began to flow without my consent. It is only in a few people's destiny to visit the holy place. People's clothing – white, a symbol of purity. The holy stone so large with gold inscriptions in Arabic. Looking at the holy water, my mind was at rest – the only real peace I had ever had in my life.

Closing thoughts

In this paraphrase of an extract from ancient Hindu writings known as *The Upanishads*, each individual is in charge of their own movement, stillness and change. The first verse will be enough for younger children to absorb initially.

Think of your body as a chariot.
Think of your thoughts as the driver.
Think of your senses as the horses.

Someone whose mind is not steady,
who does not think clearly,
and who does not feel what things really are
is like a vicious horse out of the driver's control.

But someone whose mind is steady,
who does think clearly,
and who does feel what things really are,
is like a graceful horse in the hands of a firm driver.

This traditional Irish prayer for those about to embark on a voyage might suit the occasion of a group leaving on a school journey or a residential visit, or indeed a home-time assembly.

May the road rise to meet you.
May the wind be always at your back.
May the sun shine warm upon your face,
   the rains fall soft upon your fields
   and, until we meet again,
May God hold you in the palm of his hand.

This blessing for a journey is of Amerindian origin, though the exact source is uncertain:

May your moccasins leave tracks on many mounds of worth
And walk with chiefs of every tribe who live in peace on earth.

I Go Forth to Move About the Earth

I go forth to move about the earth.
I go forth as the owl, wise and knowing.
I go forth as the eagle, powerful and bold.
I go forth as the dove, peaceful and gentle.
I go forth to move about the earth
   in wisdom, courage and peace.

(Alonzo Lopez, in Elizabeth Sulzby *et al* (eds), *This We Wish*, McGraw-Hill School Division, 1989, 0 07 042088 2, p. 307.)

A proverb, believed to be African in origin, which could be projected overhead, displayed as a banner or recited collectively.

When you have been on a journey, sit down and let your soul catch up with your body.

Mountains are very still,
they just sit and sit and sit.
They point to your greatness, O God,
silent and quiet.
Help me to be still and silent,
like a mountain,
Sitting still, listening to your voice.

(Timothy King in Louise Carpenter (ed.), *The Puffin Book of Prayers*, 1990, 0 14 034348 2, p. 74.)

Be still and know that I am God (Psalm 46:10)

3
Off and on

In many religions, light was the very first element of existence and has come to symbolise the power of creation itself. Kindling a light is a way of affirming the presence of God at the centre of life. Darkness is more than the absence of light and points to the power of the subconscious mind to cultivate whatever is unseen.

light and darkness

An activity

This poem on the mystery of light is even more powerful if realised through the following very simple ritual. Encourage as many children as possible to make candles, from new wax or melted down old, in various colours, sizes, shapes and misshapes! Cover a table or an area of floor with shiny paper (reused aluminium foil will do) and arrange the children's candles in a circle. You will also need to raid the Science resources for matches and, if the children are going to light their own candles, some tapers. Have nearby a bucket of water/sand or a fire blanket/hose in case of accident. Darken the room but station someone near the light-switch. You may also find it useful to have a small torch to follow your own script! If children are reading the poem, say, a verse each, place them behind the rest of the children so that they do not detract from the central image of the circle of light. They could memorise their verse or be issued with a small torch. It is very important for the children to be silent so that they hear the scratch of the match. Let them turn round and see the readers before they start then they will be less likely to crane their necks to see where the voices are coming from!

To read out

Spirit of Fire

1 In a circle of wax
   the candles stood round,
   awaiting the match
   that couldn't be found.
   Each separate colour
   awaited that sound –
   the all-powerful scratch of the match.

2 Rainbows of colour
   dividing the swarms
   of pure wax candles
   with too many thorns,
   varying fragrances,
   odd shapes and sizes,
   pure wax candles
   in many disguises
   stand in a circle,
   a circle of wax,
   awaiting the click
   and the scratch of the match.

3 As the match was struck
   they began to melt,
   and no one can say what pain was felt.
   The flame was revealed
   as the colours were peeled –
   and every last flame was yellow.

4 Rainbows of colour
   dividing the swarms
   of candles and people
   with too many thorns,
   varying fragrances,
   odd shapes and sizes,
   candles and people
   in human disguises
   stand in a circle,
   a circle of wax.
   As the yellow flames burn,
   the wax fills the cracks.

5 The wicks burned bright
   and softened the night;
   and hearts burned bright,
   warmed by the light;
   then slowly it dawned,
   as hearts grew mellow,
   that every last flame was yellow.

6 Rainbows of colour
  dividing the swarms
  of candles and people
  with too many thorns,
  varying fragrances,
  odd shapes and sizes,
  pure human souls
  in many disguises
  stand in a circle,
  a circle of fire,
  and human hearts burn
  with the spirit of fire.

7 Then candles were kindled
  all over the earth,
  lighting our world
  to its future re-birth,
  with yellow flames glowing
  in the hearts of men, knowing
  the kindling spirit of peace.

8 All the candles were nothing,
  nothing but tallow,
  but the spirits soared
  in flames of yellow,
  and the universe swelled
  and grew bright with light,
  as peace and love
  abolished the night.
  See through the rainbows,
  rise with the fire,
  for the universe glows
  with the spirit of fire.

(Carolyn Askar, 'Spirit of Fire' in *Spirit of Fire*, Element Books, 1983, 0 906 54043 7)

Closing thought

'O Great Chief, light a candle in my heart that I may see what is there and sweep the rubbish from your home.'

(a prayer believed to originate in Central Africa)

Mix and match

The video

Clip number 3 on the accompanying video cassette contains some very evocative material, with some quite subtle shifts of content and mood, and the children who saw it were touched with awe at the very mystery and majesty of light. Pupils may need guidance in perceiving how and why the episodes change, but this should not detract from their overall appreciation of light and darkness as human and cosmic phenomena. As in clip number 1 on page 00, they may need to see the shots separately as well as sequentially.

Everything we see is light, even in the darkness – the stars and moon, or the light that someone has turned on somewhere. Close your eyes: what can you see? Is there light inside your eyes? Or are they remembering the light you just saw in the room?

You're going to see so many kinds of light: some of them come from changes in the sky that we could never start or stop; and some come from fire that people have made.

A castle is lit up at night and against the darkness you can see the shapes of people waving enormous flags. Then the whole sky explodes with colour: whatever can that be?

Sparks are flying in the factory where machines rub metal together. Masks protect people's eyes from the sparks!

An eclipse is very rare and exciting! It happens if a planet passes in front of the moon (or even the sun). We cannot see all its light, only the dark shape of the planet against it.

Birds fly across the sun rising in the sky while a boat glides over the shining sea. Animals and just one human being cross in the dawning light. Where are they going? Darkness is always followed by the light and life begins a new day.

A long time ago in India, a demon tried to destroy Prince Rama, his wife Sita and his brother Lakhshman but Hanuman and all the monkey kingdom drove the demon out,

making the world safe for them. At the beginning of winter, Hindus celebrate the festival of Diwali to show that goodness can make badness go away just as light can make darkness go away.

Lourdes is a special place in France where a young nun called Bernadette once had a vision of the Virgin Mary, the mother of Jesus. On that spot there is a spring of water and some Christians who are sick or disabled come thousands of miles to touch or drink the water which they believe will cure them. By candlelight, they are singing 'Ave Maria' (Hail Mary).

This Jewish family is celebrating the festival of Hanukah for eight nights and remembering what happened to their people long ago: an army marched into Israel, destroyed their Temple, spilt their everlasting lamp and tried to make them worship their own cruel king instead of God. A tiny bit of oil the Jews had burned for eight days until they found more. That's why there are eight candles! They eat potato latkes fried in oil and sing how God is a rock who makes people strong inside.

A fuller account of the Rama and Sita story will develop children's appreciation of the central theme. It is available in many versions but the most vivid are:

Rani and Jugnu Singh, *The Amazing Adventures of Hanuman*, BBC, 1988, 0 563 21425 2 – simply told and dynamically illustrated, especially for younger children.

Ruskin Bond, *The Adventures of Rama and Sita*, Walker Books, 1987, 0 744 51445 2. Episodes of the Ramayana epic retold in considerable detail and modern language for older children.

To read out

This extract may helpfully extend the focus on Diwali:

Kamla and Kate are best friends at school. At playtime, Kamla has been trying to balance a stone on the palm of her hand and then twist her hand round in circles. She tells Kate that it is going to be a surprise! Kamla's family, who are Hindu, invite Kate's family to a Diwali party and as they draw near they are enchanted by the small saucers of glowing lights on every window sill and the garden path lined with flickering flames from sparkling wicks dipped in oil. Inside, there were more diwas of oil with wicks on the mantelpiece and in every niche. The lights made the gold and silver threads of the women's saris glisten . . . the sequins and beads on Kamla's costume flash . . . the jewellery gleam brightly . . .

. . . Kate suddenly caught sight of her friend. This was a really big surprise. Kamla was dressed up as a dancing girl . . . Her eyes were outlined in black; she had a red mark in the middle of her forehead, and the palms of her hands were painted red too. There were jangling bells round her ankles and glass bangles tinkled on her wrists.

'Mum! Look at Kamla!' cried Kate in astonishment. Everyone looked surprised. Even Kamla's mother and father.

'Kamla has been secretly learning a very special dance for Diwali,' announced Leela, leading her little cousin into the centre of the circle . . . 'Kamla will now dance a temple dance in which she offers a gift of light to the god.' Then Leela stepped over to the mantelpiece and took down a very small saucer with a softly burning light. She placed it on the palm of Kamla's outstretched hand.

'So that's what she was practising so secretly,' hissed Kate. 'I hope she doesn't drop it!'

First Kamla stood like a statue with the flame burning in her hand. Then, as the accordion breathed out its tune, and the bells clashed a rhythm, she stamped first one foot then the other. Gradually she began to move round, gliding gracefully so as not to upset the saucer of flame. She swayed this way and that, raising the saucer from one side to the other.

Then came the really hard bit. Kate could hardly bear to look. Kamla began to twist her palm round as she had done in the playground. Would she drop the saucer? Would she get burnt by the flame as it twisted under? No one dared make a sound. Kamla twisted the saucer on her palm round . . . and round . . . and round . . . while she gradually dropped lower and lower to the ground. At last she was kneeling and brought the saucer in its last circle down to the ground. She placed it like an offering in the middle of the room.

Everyone burst out cheering and clapping. 'Shabash!' they shouted. 'Well done!' What a secret! Kate didn't know, and not even Kamla's mother had known.

(Jamila Gavin, *Kamla and Kate*, Magnet, 1983, 0 416 50450 7, pp. 106–8)

To read out or act

Book box

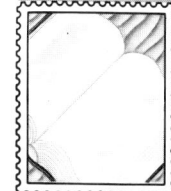

The festival of Hanukah can be developed with the children through any or all of the following:

Judye Groner and Madeline Wikler, *All About Hanukkah*, Kar-ben Copies, 1988, 0 930 49482 2 – stories, recipes, games, songs . . .

Yehuda and Sara Wurtzel, *Lights: a Fable about Hanukah*, Rossel Books, 1985, 0 940 64656 0. An evocative account of Hanukah's origins: light symbolises revelation, tradition and identity.

Floreva G. Cohen, *A Hanukkiyah for Dina*, Board of Jewish Education of N.Y., 1980; no ISBN but available in Britain.

Eileen Sherman, *The Odd Potato*, Kar-ben Copies, 1984, 0 930 49437 7. It was the first Hanukah since Rachel's mother had died: she couldn't find the hanukiyah and her father seemed too sad to bother, so she improvised with a large, funnily shaped potato.

Barbara Goldin, *Just Enough is Plenty*, Heinemann, 1988, 0 434 93496 8. A stranger comes to the door of a poor Jewish home and is made welcome.

This story has been variously attributed but this version owes its origin to the people of Helm, who are noted, in Jewish legend, for their excess of wit yet lack of wisdom. It dramatises effectively, painlessly and to the point the reading below.

A man was kneeling down under a lamp-post, leaning slightly forward and feeling the ground all around when along came his sister.

'What on earth are you doing groping the ground like that? Do you need any help?'

'Yes, thank you. I've lost my key!'

With that, his kind sister got down on her knees and started looking for the key, too. After a few minutes, when they'd had no luck, she asked him, 'Haven't you got any idea where you dropped it? Try and remember!'

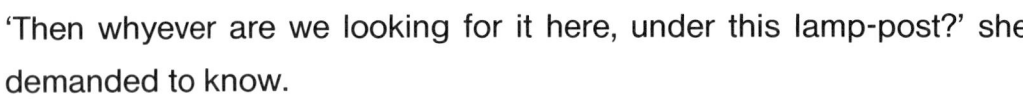
'Oh, I know exactly where I lost it,' he replied. 'In my house!'

'Then whyever are we looking for it here, under this lamp-post?' she demanded to know.

'Because there's more light here!'

. . . .

The song

New Year Song

This traditional Chinese New Year song was transmitted by Christine Chin. The music was transcribed by Walter Robson and the transliteration and the English version were written by Angela Wood.

(If 'tch' is difficult to pronounce, 'ch' as in 'chicken' is an approximation. 'Chay' rhymes with 'apple pie'.)

Book box

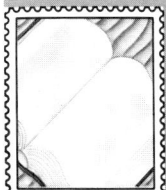

Rumer Godden, *Fu-Dog*, Walker Books, 1989, 0 862 03368 3. Li-la and her bother Malcolm are half-Chinese and they run away with Fu-Dog, an ornamental satin dog.

Eve Rice, *Goodnight, Goodnight*, Picture Puffins, 1983, 0 140 50386 2. A satisfying book in shades of black, white and yellow, for the very young.

Reeve Lindbergh, *The Midnight Farm*, Picture Puffins, 1987, 0 140 50887 2. A counting book of rhyming couplets.

Saviour Pirotta, *Let the Shadows Fly*, Hamish Hamilton, 1986, 0 241 11800 X. Inside a hideout which twelve children have built on the common, they dig for a treasure chest and find four ancient candles.

Karen Acherman, *The Banshee*, Philomel Books, 1990, 0 399 21924 2. When the darkness has left no place for light to hide, the banshee searches for a lonely soul to keep her company.

Jill Tomlinson, *The Owl who was Afraid of the Dark*, Puffin Books, 1987, 0 140 30634 X. Though not a picture story book, the seven well-loved and now famous chapters are very suitable for reading aloud even to the quite young.

M. Christina Butler, *Stanley in the Dark*, Simon and Schuster, 1990, 0 750 00220 4. A mouse mistakes the moon for a round cheese.

Donna Reid Vann, *Stefan's Secret Fear*, Lion, 1990, 0 745 91307 5. Stefan seems courageous, but is afraid of the dark and afraid that people will find out.

Suzanne Bukiet, 'The Eclipse of the Sun: an Indian Tale' in *Scripts*, Mantra Publishing, 1989, 1 852 69094 1. Kantra loses her parents in a forest and is raised by a gentle tigress.

Moira Kemp, *The Firebird*, Hamish Hamilton, 1983, 0 241 10810 1. A gloriously illustrated story from Czechoslovakia.

An activity

A human circle of light can be achieved simply but effectively by selecting published poetry, verses from scriptures or children's writing on the theme of light and having them read in the darkness, with a single beam shining on each reader in turn. Elaborate spotlights are not necessary: a large flashlight will produce the same effect. The selection will need to be tailor-made but this is a 'starter pack':

Closing thoughts

'If they are blind, give them your hand.
If they are in the dark, give them a candle.'
(source unknown)

'It is better to light one candle than to curse the multitude of darkness.'
(source unknown)

'The best and most beautiful things in the world cannot be seen or heard. They must be felt in the heart.'
(Helen Keller, blind and deaf from birth)

'Jesus said . . . "I am the light of the world; anyone who follows me will not walk in darkness, but will have the light of life."'
(from the Christian New Testament)

'I stood in a roomful of shadows,
Silent,
Waiting,
For myself.

'I stood in a roomful of mirrors,
Moving,
Looking,
For myself.

'I stood in a roomful of light,
Blinking,
Smiling,
For myself.'

(Peter Cunningham, age 15, in Chris Searle (ed.), *Fire Words*, Jonathan Cape, 1972, 0 224 00776 9, p. 33)

4 Splash!

As the basis for all life, water may have been the original habitat for all creatures. The very quality and texture of water make it difficult to define or control, and water in nature seems to express a wide range of moods. In religious rituals, water variously symbolises purity, refreshment, continuity and renewal.

water

Activities

There is a range of possible starting-points on this theme:

Bring together a number of objects associated with water, such as an umbrella, ice-tray, watering-can or toy boat. Ask very young children to name them and guess the connection; or put the objects in a 'feely box'; or ask children to identify them while blindfolded, aided and abetted by the non-blindfolded.

Hum well-known nursery rhymes, popular songs or themes from classical music on the theme of water, such as 'Incy-wincy spider', 'It's raining, it's pouring', 'Raindrops keep falling on my head', 'Ice', 'Water Music' or 'The Blue Danube'. Ask the children to identify the tunes and spot the theme.

Begin with a riddle or two and ask for the unifying element:

Q. What runs all day and night, without stopping?
A. *A river.*

Q. What fish swims through water like lightning?
A. *The sting ray.*

Q. What does a sea monster have for pudding?
A. *Jelly fish.*

Q. How do you cut the sea in half?
A. *With a sea saw.*

Q. What did the ground say to the rain?
A. *If you don't stop hitting me, my name will be mud.*

The video

Through four sequences, clip number 4 on the accompanying video cassette conveys much of the power and potential of water that will be immediately apparent to the children. Water is the basis of all creation, a natural resource and an important element in human life. If you can, show and discuss each sequence separately as well as taking the clip as a whole (see notes on clip number 1 on page 18).

Everything that lives needs water – plants, all kinds of animals and people. What do you use water for? Why is wasting water wrong? How does it look . . . sound . . . taste . . . smell . . . feel . . . ? Is water always the same? Can you make it do what you want? Can you think of a nickname for water?

What comes into your mind when you think of the seaside? Look at the waves crashing onto the shore! Is that what you imagined? People can build walls to try and stop the sea flooding the land, but they can never stop the sea itself because it has its own power! There is a legend about a king called Canute who was so bossy that people said he could make the sea turn back just by telling it to. One day, he stood on the beach when the sea was very stormy and told the waves to go back. What do you think happened?

We all use water to wash ourselves when we're dirty and there's something we want to get off us. People often have something in them or about them that they want to get off and sometimes when people become Christians they are baptised by being plunged into water to feel they are starting a new life, all clean inside them. What also makes it important for Christians is that Jesus was baptised (about 2000 years ago). Why do you think some Christians go to Israel to be baptised in the same river?

What makes this river run so fast? Is it only the water's own power? Do you fancy a joyride in a wooden tub on the rapids?

Compare the sea here with the sea at the beginning. The fish might like it better rough because then the gulls couldn't dive in and catch them for a tasty meal!

Closing thoughts

This is what three eight-year-olds thought about water:

'Everything that water does – except for floods and children drowning – is good for us.'
(Sivan Greene)

'Water is just like humans because its moods change.'
(Ester Gluck)

'Water flows
Water goes
When the wind blows!'
(Thomas Bush)

Mix and match

An activity

Show the children a jug of water, some ice cubes and a steaming kettle and, pointing to each one in turn, ask if it is water. Explain that water can take the form of liquid, solid or vapour and that they are *all* water.

Explore with the children the fact that people can also be seen in more than one way and have more than one name. You might use yourself as an exemplar, choosing, say, three roles you play, something like this: 'I am a teacher and you all call me Mr/Ms . . . but I am also a mother/father and my children call me . . . My friend calls me . . . or so-and-so has a special name for me: it is a secret!'

Such diversity of name and role is at the heart of many religious teachings about God. It is perhaps too sophisticated to introduce the concepts to the children, yet many have discovered it themselves and spontaneously shared the insight.

Book box

Robert Roennfeldt, *Tiddalick*, Picture Puffins, 1988, 0 14 050349 8. Tiddalick was a frog with a huge thirst who drank up all the seas and rivers.

Verna Aardema, *Bimwali and the Zimwi*, Hamish Hamilton, 1986, 0 241 11883 2. A little girl realises that, on the beach where she was playing with her sisters, she has left behind a special shell.

Verna Aardema, *Bringing the Rain to Kapiti Plain*, Macmillan, 1986, 0 333 35164 9. A cumulative poem in rhyming couplets based on a traditional Kenyan tale of a young man who shot a cloud to bring down the rain!

David McKee, *The Day the Tide Went Out . . . And Out . . .* , Blackie, 1985, 0 216 91740 9. The beachkeeper hated it when the animals from the jungle built sandcastles on his back while he was snoozing!

John Burningham, *Come away from the water, Shirley*, Picture Lions, 1983, 0 00 662147 3. Too cold for swimming, the day at the beach is spent by Shirley's parents reading the newspaper and preventing her from having fun.

John Burningham, *Time to get out of the bath, Shirley*, Picture Lions, 1985, 0 00 662393 X. When the water is let out, Shirley floats down the plug-hole and finds the sea of her imagination.

The cassette

The story 'Water is a strange thing' on the accompanying audio cassette is an African creation myth in which the Great God sent his only son to earth to see if it was fit to live on. There was no water and it was so hot that he crawled into a crack in the rock and was never seen again. So God then sent the first woman and the first man to find him – but in vain. Yet God was so pleased with their efforts that he gave them the earth to live in as a reward and he sent rain on to the earth. In the water, they can see a reflection of the face of God.

To read out

In this story of the Sufi tradition (that of Islamic mysticism), water is precious because it is in short supply and has come to symbolise the delights of heaven.

The Bedouin people live in tents in the desert and wander from place to place, wherever their cattle graze. It is very hard indeed for them to find clean water and the little that they have they keep very carefully.

One day a Bedouin couple were invited by the sultan to his palace which was a great honour. To show how thankful they were, they decided to give him a really nice present. What was the very best thing they had? A small pot of water! It was a little dirty but it was still their most valued possession so they decided to present it to him as soon as they arrived . . . though there was something about his palace that they didn't know . . .

Gently they carried the pot together across the hot desert sands, being very careful not to spill a single drop of the precious liquid. As they got near to the palace, the rich man saw them coming and was curious about what they were holding; so he sent his servants to find out what it was . . . ●

The sultan was horrified when he heard the news. 'Are you quite sure it's water they're bringing? Surely not all this way . . . Oh dear! How awful!' Then he called to the doorkeeper, 'Quick! Don't let them come the front way, whatever happens: send them round the back!'

Minutes later, the couple trudged the long way round to the rear entrance and were finally let in. As soon as they saw the sultan, they bowed low and offered their pot of dirty water. Their host gave them such a warm smile and thanked them so deeply for the treasure they had given him, that they felt wonderful all over . . . *so* wonderful that when they left to go home, they didn't even notice the stream of fresh clear water that ran past the front of the sultan's home!

The song

Come, Rain!

From Bengali folk tradition, this is a desperate but positive cry for much-needed rain. The song was transmitted and transliterated by Indira Sen; the music transcribed by Keith Lovell; and the English version written by Angela Wood.

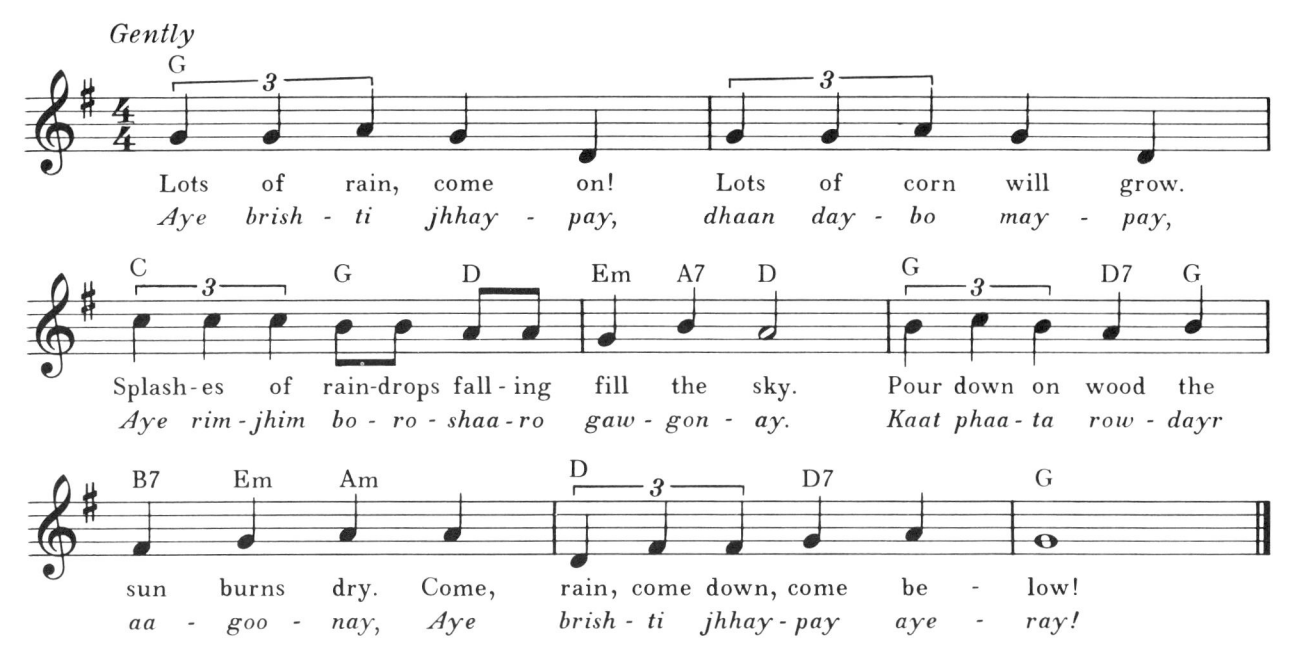

Gently

Lots of rain, come on! Lots of corn will grow.
Aye brish-ti jhhay-pay, dhaan day-bo may-pay,

Splash-es of rain-drops fall-ing fill the sky. Pour down on wood the
Aye rim-jhim bo-ro-shaa-ro gaw-gon-ay. Kaat phaa-ta row-dayr

sun burns dry. Come, rain, come down, come be - low!
aa - goo - nay, Aye brish - ti jhhay - pay aye - ray!

To read out or act

This enacted parable derives from the life of Svetaketu, a young Hindu whose father suspects him of being arrogant and superficial, and so demonstrates that the Pure Being, Brahman, fills the whole universe and cannot be separated from it.

The parable is simple and fun to act out. You will need a glass of water, some table salt, and something to tip into!

The boy's father gives him some salt and asks him to put it in a glass of water and bring it to him the next day.

In the morning the father asks the boy for the salt but he cannot give it as it has all dissolved.

'Take a sip of the water and tell me what it tastes like!' the man tells the boy.

'It's salty!'

'Pour some away,' his father goes on, 'and taste it again!'

'It's still salty!'

'Right, now pour it all away and taste from the bottom of the glass.'

'It's still salty!'

'You see,' said the father, 'the Pure Being cannot be taken out of the world but is still there . . .'

Closing thought

The Zambezi is a strong river running through Central Africa:

'Make us move together like Zambezi, Lord,
As we journey through this trying world.
Make us peaceful and shining, dear God,
But strong enough within – with your word –
To smash Satan's barriers on our road.
Thus as Zambezi surely reaches the sea,
So may we finally your Kingdom see.'

(Anonymous, in Leprosy Mission 'New Day', number 339, p. 20)

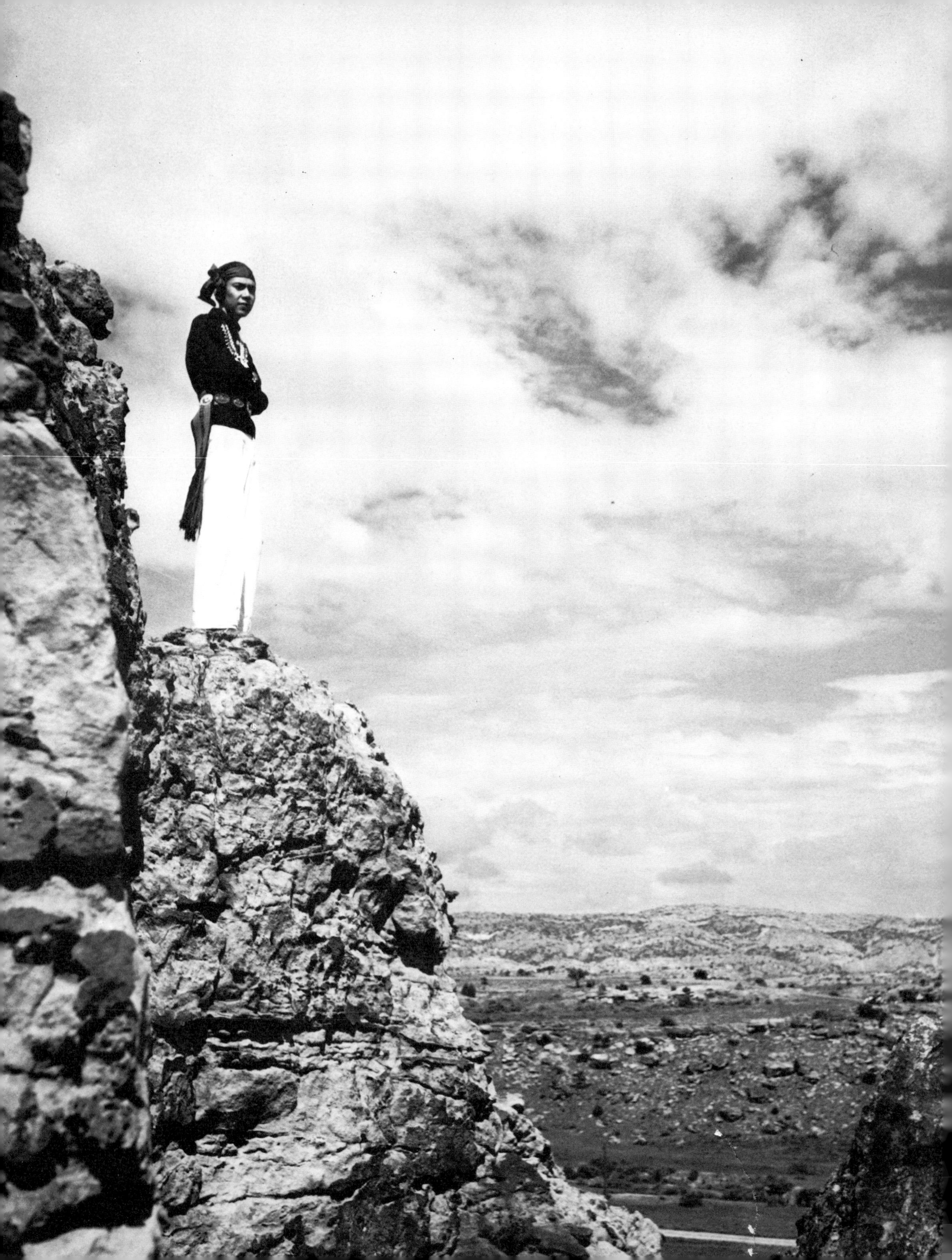

5

Blowing in the wind

Modern life, even in the countryside, has torn us away from the rhythm of the earth and the cycle of the seasons. In searching for our roots, we can feel again that we belong with the earth and her creatures.

harmony with nature

The experience of Noah's Ark superficially seems to belong in a water theme. Yet in reality it does not greatly extend children's understanding of the quality, role and imagery of water and is not really *about* water at all, but about the way in which our environment can smile or frown. It is little wonder that the story has inspired the brand-name of a company making ecologically sound cleaning materials! The whole experience seems to lie more profoundly at the heart of the question: how are we linked to our world and to God?

Book box

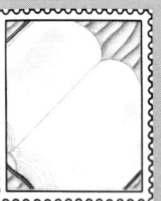

Countless versions of the story abound and it also seems to have inspired much commercial art, including teatowels!

Gertrude Fussenegger, *Noah's Ark*, Hodder and Stoughton, 1984, 0 340 28629 6. Conveys an ancient feel through language, though the full-colour illustrations are medieval in tone and texture.

Peter Spier, *The Great Flood*, Purnell, 1979, 0 437 76512 1. Is text-free with detailed illustrations to intrigue young children for hours.

Variations on the theme also abound and two deserve mention:

Roger Smith, *How the Animals Saved the Ark and Put Two and Two Together*, Picture Puffins, 1988, 0 14 050918 6 is a mathematical treatment with some painful puns and Mrs Noah in a central role.

Ann and Reg Cartwright, *Norah's Ark*, Picture Puffins, 1988, 0 14 050477 X. The pond is too small for all the animals that Norah keeps and they have to take it in turns for the water. Then comes the flood and they sail away in an upturned barn! As the waters subside, they see that the flood has left the biggest ever pond!

To read out

It is important that children know what a limbo dance is in order to understand this poem: you may need to demonstrate!

Rainbow

When you see
de rainbow
you know
God know
wha he doing –
one big smile
across the sky –
I tell you
God got style
the man got style

When you see
raincloud pass
and de rainbow
make a show
I tell you
is God doing
limbo
the man doing limbo

But sometimes
you know
when I see
de rainbow
so full of glow
and curving
like she bearing child
I does want know
if God
ain't a woman

If that is so
the woman got style
man she got style.

(John Agard, 'Rainbow' in *Mangoes and Bullets*, Pluto Press, 1985, 0 7453 0028 6, p. 27)

To read out

A Jewish legend which explores and extends the biblical story:

As Noah's family and the animals were entering the ark, Lie rushed up at the last minute. 'Can I get on? PLEASE!'

'Sorry!' Noah answered. 'We're only taking couples!'

'Just a minute, then,' cried Lie. 'I'll be right back!' And with that he went off to find Evil.

'You are the only one for me,' Lie swore to Evil. 'Let us be married and sail away!' Evil was so flattered at the proposal of marriage that she agreed and, just a second before the gangplank was pulled up, they slithered on in two-by-two style... though Noah was far from pleased! ●

After forty days, when it was safe for all the creatures to leave the ark for dry land again, Noah reminded them of God's promise never to destroy the world again. He pointed to the rainbow in the sky as a sign of that promise and told all the creatures that their side of the bargain was to increase and multiply, to have children for generation after generation.

'All' unfortunately included Lie and Evil and in that they obeyed – spreading their offspring over all the earth and spoiling our lives with the things that God had wanted to destroy in the first place.

(An illustrated version of this story is told in Sybil Sheridan, *Stories from the Jewish World*, Macdonald, 1987, 0 356 11562 3, pp. 12f.)

Closing thought

According to a Jewish tradition, God said to Noah when the flood was over:

Take care of our world; for if you spoil it, there will be no one after you to set it right.

(This may serve as a mantra, a repeated saying, displayed if possible for all to see.)

Mix and match

The cassette

The 'Everglades' story on the accompanying audio cassette is set in an imaginary place of gnarled roots, twisting creepers and frondy leaves. There live bird-like creatures called 'preeners' whose enemies are the river warts. The White Bird came to sing but did not stay long and the song is soon forgotten. One night the preeners cross to the forbidden side of the river but they begin to sink and to save themselves they try to recall the song. As dawn breaks, the song comes back to them as though the White Bird were singing it with them . . .

The video

Although clip number 5 on the accompanying video cassette is removed from our children's everyday experiences, it is effective to show it with little or no introduction and allow the harmony of wind and movement, of colour and clouds, of music and flags, of people and birds to reach the children directly. They bubble with questions afterwards!

A Buddhist community in a mountainous region of Bhutan sets up 'prayer flags' – cloths on which they have written texts – to catch the breeze and cast their meditations into the universe. Dancers in vivid costume spin rhythmically to a beat that becomes almost hypnotic, and we catch glimpses of the flapping cloths and the homing birds as though there were three realms of meaning that had for a moment become one. Then all is still.

To read out

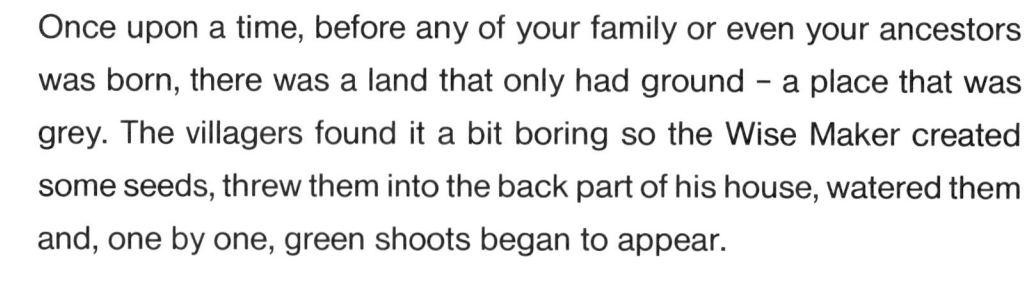

Once upon a time, before any of your family or even your ancestors was born, there was a land that only had ground – a place that was grey. The villagers found it a bit boring so the Wise Maker created some seeds, threw them into the back part of his house, watered them and, one by one, green shoots began to appear.

Everyone was really glad to have a bit of colour even though it was not everywhere. So they asked the Wise Maker, 'How do you do this? Could you show us how to get the green shoots in the back part of our house?' ●

And he said, 'Sure!' and he showed them how to do it and gave them seeds.

They planted them in the back of their houses and did the same as him when all of a sudden the place – and not just the back but everywhere! – was full of these green shoots. Everyone was really happy to have green but after a while they called out, 'Hey! We're getting a bit bored, you know, because we're just looking at green!'

The Wise Maker said, 'All right! Point taken!' So he made some more seeds, planted them and watered them just like the others. And what do you think happened? They grew into colourful things. After a while the people said, 'What shall we call them? Let's start with the green shoots!' ▲

'They're *green*!' said the Wise Maker, 'and they grow out of the *ground* so they should begin with a "gr" sound.' Then out of the blue he said, 'Let's call them "grass"!'

'What are we going to call the colourful other shoots?'

'You know "wolf"? Well, backwards it is "flow". So if "flow" is the opposite of "wolf" and "wolf" is angry, "flow" must be nice. Now these flow are even nicer than lots of nice things so we'll call them flow-er!'

The Wise Maker called a village meeting and everyone agreed so they did it. They had one final problem and they thought if the Wise Maker solved this he would be famous all over the world: they wanted to know what to call the back part of their house. The Wise Maker said, 'It will be lovely but not as lovely as the Garden of Eden so just call it "garden" with flowers and grass.'

(Ester Gluck, age 7)

The song

Let the Heavens Shout

(The pronunciation of 'ay' rhymes with 'pie'. The 'h' in 'yis'-m'-hu' sounds like the Scottish 'loch' or the Welsh 'bach'.)

The Hebrew words are taken from the Jewish prayer book and the melody is traditional. The English version was written by Angela Wood.

Joyfully

Let the hea-vens shout for joy, Let the hea-vens shout for joy,
Yis'- m'- hu ha - sha - ma - yim, Yis'- m'- hu ha - sha - ma - yim,

Let the hea-vens shout for_ joy___ And let the earth sing and be glad! glad!
Yis'- m'- hu ha - sha - ma - yi - (i)m V'- tar - gel_ ha'- a - retz. retz.

Let the sea fill out, Let the sea fill out, Let the sea fill out_ And_
Yir - am ha-yam, Yir - am ha-yam, Yir - am ha-ya - (a)m_

yell and roar! yell and roar! Let the sea fill out, Let the sea fill out,
Oom - lo' - o. Oom - lo' - o. Yir - am ha-yam, Yir - am ha-yam,

Let the sea fill out_ And_ yell and roar! yell and roar! Let the sea fill out,
Yir - am ha-ya - (a)m_ Oom - lo' - o. Oom - lo' - o. Yir - am ha-yam,

D.C. al Fine

Let the sea fill out, Let the sea fill out_ And_ yell and roar! yell and roar!
Yir - am ha-yam, Yir - am ha-ya - (a)m_ Oom - lo' - o. Oom - lo' - o.

Book box

Angela Wood, 'A World of His Own' in *Faith Stories for Today*, BBC/Longman, 1990, 0 582 05946 1. Guru Nanak, the first of the ten Sikh gurus, loved to commune with nature. One day he seemed to go into a trance and had a near miss!

Michael Foreman, *One World*, Anderson Press, 1990, 0 86264 289 2. A sensitive book about two children playing by the seashore, in touch with nature, and pondering the delicate relationships between all living things.

Janet and Allan Ahlberg, *The Worm Book*, Picture Lions, 1989, 0 00 663361 7. A light-hearted appreciation of this otherwise 'lowly' creature and a simple tribute to the earth itself.

Eric Carle, *The Very Quiet Cricket*, Hamish Hamilton, 1990, 0 241 12985 0, a literally audible book!

Oscar Wilde, 'The Selfish Giant' presented in the form of recorded reading with a song, booklet of text and picture cards by July Days and Jim Wingate, Friendly Press, 1987, 0 948728 15 9.

Closing thoughts

This poem of Rabindranath Tagore was translated by Radha Krishnamoorthi when she was 17. The first two verses are strictly about nature and they may be enough for the children to do the exercise, anyway.

Close your eyes and I will read you a poem written by an Indian man a long time ago. He is asking God to make the world the way it should be. Pretend that you have a paint-brush in your hand and there is a piece of paper propped up in the air. As I read to you, paint what you can see in your mind. Keep your eyes shut or your painting will be ruined. If you're still painting when I finish, I'll read the poem again.

Let the earth and the water, the air and the fruits of the land be sweet, my God.

Let the homes and markets, the forests and fields of the land be full, my God.

Let the promises and hopes, the acts and words of my people be true, my God.

Let the lives and hearts of the sons and daughters of my people be one, my God.

Teach your children what we have taught our children: that the earth is our true mother. Whatever happens to the earth, happens to the children of the earth. If people spit on the ground, they spit on themselves.

We know: the earth does not belong to people but people belong to the earth.

We know: everything is joined together in some way, like the blood that runs through a family.

Everything is joined together. Whatever happens to the earth, happens to the children of the earth. We did not weave the web of life; we are just a strand in it. Whatever we do to the web, we do to ourselves.

(An historic address given by the Amerindian leader, Chief Seattle, to the 'white man'; a modified call and response effect is achieved through alternating readers.)

Glory be to that God that is in the fire,
Who is in the water,
Who is in the trees,
Who is in all things in this huge world.
To that Spirit be glory!

(A Hindu prayer from the Svetasvatara Upanishad)

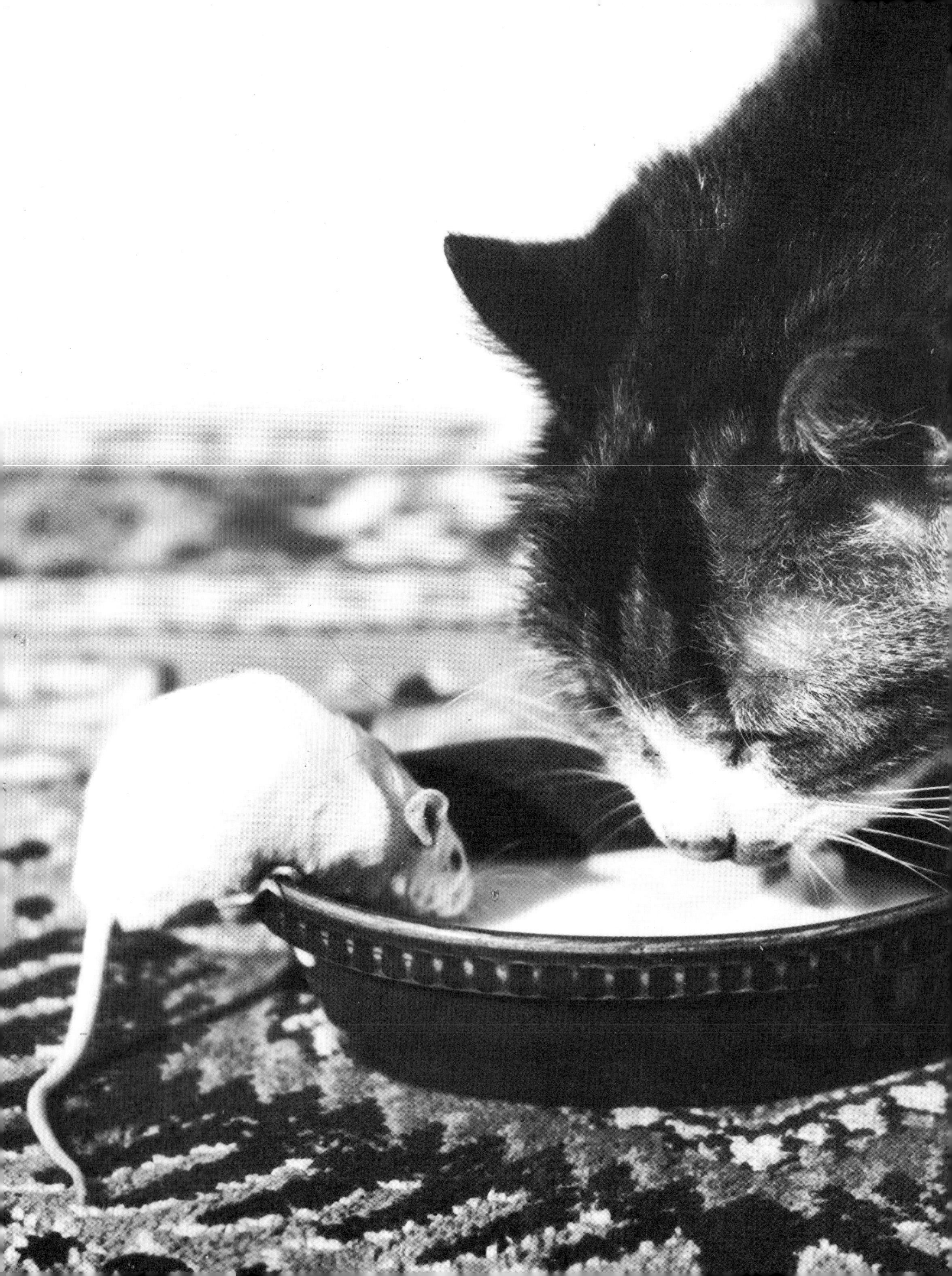

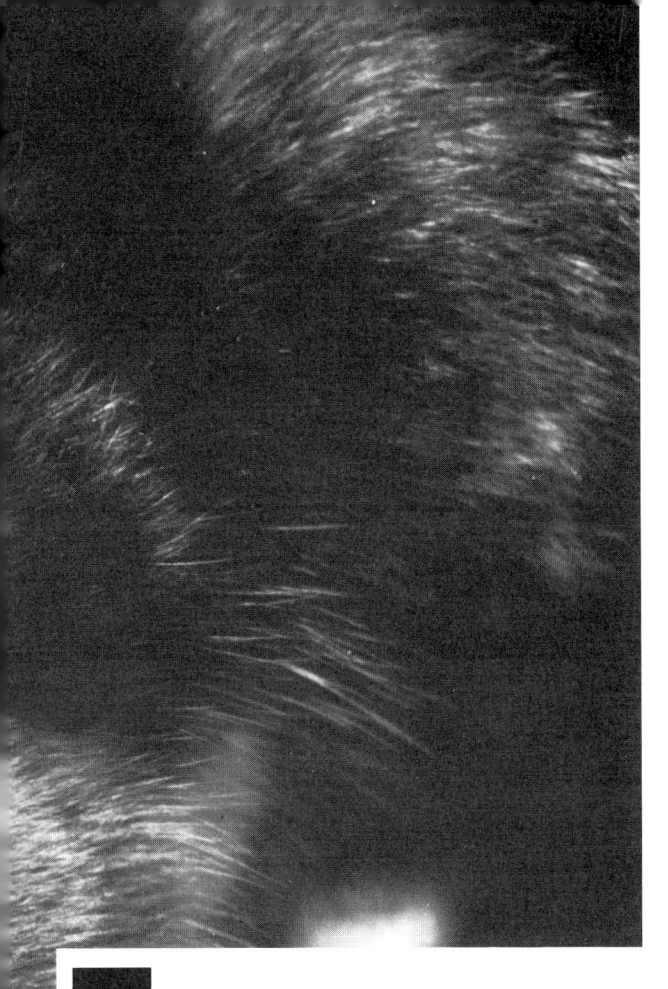

6

The world in our hands

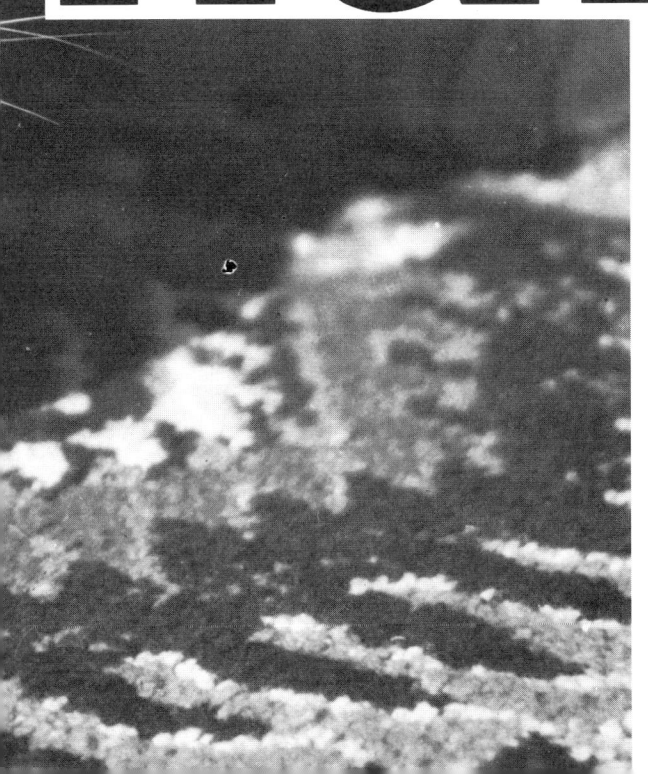

We take a lot from other creatures in the world and from nature as a whole. What do we have to offer? And what can we do to repair the harm we have caused?

caring for the natural world

The video

Clip number 6 on the accompanying video cassette shows that the threat to the rainforests is somehow synonymous with the threat to nature itself, and has rightly become a *cause célèbre*. Rainforests house numerous and diverse species of plants and animals, and have provided a supportive, healthy environment for the peoples who have traditionally lived there. The problems have been imported by greedy governments and money-mad manufacturers who have exploited and subdued the rainforests, creating devastation and disease.

Perhaps the rainforests will seem to you like a magic jungle from a fairy tale with so many marvellous kinds of plants and animals that will grow and live for ever. But the rainforests are *real* and they could *stay* real if people didn't spoil them: people coming from cities far away using wood-cutting machines and big bull-dozers to cut down the beautiful trees and dig up the ground, burning what's left! Imagine how scared the animals are when this happens! And how sad when their homes and food are gone! It harms the people who live there, too, because the wonderful world they know is going; they are not used to the city people's ways and it makes them sick!

Book box

Helen Cowcher, *Rainforest*, Picture Corgi, 1990, 0 552 525537. Dazzling colour and the stark, bold text make this an utterly memorable book about any and every rainforest, especially for young children.

Jeannie Baker, *Where the Forest Meets the Sea*, Walker, 1989, 0 7445 1305 7. An innovative picture book charting a young boy's exploration of prehistoric rainforests in Australia and his anxiety for their future.

Lynne Cherry, *The Great Kapok Tree*, Harcourt Brace Jovanovich, 1990, 0 15 200520 X. Subtitled 'A Tale of the Amazon Rain Forest', this is a haunting book about a treechopper who falls asleep in the forest.

Closing thought

This is suitable for reciting together and display:

'God had no big building in the garden of Paradise, only animals, birds, fruit and flowers.'

(Marian Smart, age 10, Nigeria; Helen Exley (ed.), *Cry for our Beautiful World* Exley Publications, 1985, 1 85015 010 9, p. 51)

Mix and match

To read out or act

Ask the children to put themselves in the position of the judge in this Buddhist story and decide what should happen to the swan:

'Goodness me!' said the judge. 'This poor wounded swan can't belong to both of you! But you say she's yours, Devadetta?'

'Certainly!' replied Devadetta. 'I shot it and it fell so I must have nearly killed her – so she's mine.'

'That seems clear enough . . . what do you have to say, Siddhartha?'

'That beautiful swan suddenly fell injured at my feet as I was out walking. I could see that someone had shot it with an arrow which I pulled out very gently. Then I soothed the poor creature in my arms until she fell asleep.'

(The verdict of the judge in the story: it is better to save life than to kill, therefore the swan belongs to Siddhartha.)

Book box

'Out of the Ark' and 'The Green Page' stimulate informed discussion on ecological questions and are regular features of *Early Times*, a weekly journal ("The independent newspaper for young people") which is published by Garth Publications Ltd, Brighton Business Centre, 95 Ditchling Road, Brighton BN1 4SE, and is available through local newsagents.

John Burningham, *Oi! Get Off Our Train*, Jonathan Cape, 1989, 0 224 02698 4. A boy is playing with his train set just before bedtime and, in his dreams, he is an engine-driver who initially tries to prevent endangered species from coming aboard.

Jeanne Titherington, *Pumpkin, Pumpkin*, Picture Piper, 1986, 0 330 30093 8. A simple invitation to the process of growth, responsibility and hope.

Shel Silverstein, *The Giving Tree*, Harper and Row, 1984, 0 06 025666 4. A tree indulges a little boy in all his games and pleasures.

Michael Foreman, *Dinosaurs and all that rubbish*, Picture Puffins, 1988, 0 14 050098 7. A humorous and meaningful fable of modern life.

The song

Growing Up

This song was based on the story of the same title by Angela Wood in *Faith Stories for Today*, BBC/Longman, 1990, 0 582 05946 1, pp. 16–21. That in turn is a modern adaptation of the Christian parable of the talents, whereby three gardeners are entrusted with seeds, not coins.

The words and music of the song were specially composed for *Assembly Kit* by Stephen Clark and the music was transcribed by Kate Buchanan.

A steel band arrangement would be ideal but any percussion, particularly shakers, maracas, cabasas and so on would help to give the song a calypso feel.

Calypso rhythm

1. Now there's a park in the middle of town
Where people go to play,
To read and talk and think and walk,
To dream their life away.
And people go there all day long
Until it's getting dark.
It's the place you know all the flowers grow
And it's run by Super-park.

Chorus
This is where we see
If they all agree,
And if all three
Will hear the plea.
And you and me,
Would we all agree?
If the choice was free,
What would it be?

54

2. Now Superpark had a meeting in town
   And had to go off site.
   The gardeners said, 'Just go ahead',
   That everything would be all right.
   Then Superpark gave them some seeds,
   And left them with this thought:
   'When I return then I shall learn
   Who's listened to what I've taught.'

3. Now Grow Bag knew just what to do
   That soon it would be done,
   'I'll sprinkle them around on the open ground
   And then I'll have some fun.'
   But Greenfingers worked hard all week
   With hoe and fork and spade,
   Till the seeds were sown and the shoots were grown
   And the flower bed was made.

4. But Flower Pot knew that the seeds were safe
   Under lock and key
   And Flower Pot's fear they would disappear
   Wouldn't let them free.
   And Grow Bag's seeds were doing well
   While Grow Bag played and played,
   But you might have guessed that the seeds most blessed
   Were the ones Greenfingers laid.

   This is where we see
   If they all agree,
   And if all three
   Will hear the plea.
   And you and me,
   Would we all agree?
   If the choice was free
   What would it be?

5. When Superpark came back to see their work
   And saw the flower bed,
   Looking around at the beautiful ground
   This is what was said:
   'Now, Grow Bag, yours are doing well,
   They make a good display.
   Maybe there'd be more if you'd stuck to your chore
   But everybody needs to play.'

6. 'But Greenfingers, I'm really very proud,
   Just look at what you've done.
   This will bring joy to every girl and boy
   And pleasure to everyone.
   And Flower Pot I understand,
   Why you hid them so,
   But seeds are seeds with special needs:
   Yes, seeds are meant to grow.'

   This is where we see
   If they all agree,
   And if all three
   Will hear the plea.
   And you and me,
   Would we all agree?
   If the choice was free
   What would it be?

To read out

This Hindu story about Krishna, an incarnation of God, shows how high animals come in the order of things. Pause as you approach a word or phrase in brackets and allow the children to suggest what it contains: this will increase powers of concentration, help them to focus on the meaning they are making and heighten the enjoyment of anticipation.

All the soldiers were lined up, waiting for the orders and the elephant drivers had scrambled up to the necks of the (*beasts*). The archers were ready, each one with an (*arrow*) in place in a (*bow*). The charioteers were listening for the call to (*advance*) and soon the conch shell would (*sound*) to say that the (*battle*) was beginning.

Krishna suddenly noticed a bird (*fluttering*) beside the (*soldiers*) in the middle of the (*battlefield*). He couldn't understand why it hadn't (*flown*) away from the (*noise*) and (*smoke*) of the enemy camps. The little lapwing was darting about in the (*air*) and (*twittering*) sweetly just above a clump of (*grass*) that Krishna thought she must have made a nest in it. Oh dear! It could be very (*dangerous*) for the little (*birds*). So guess what he did! He lifted a heavy elephant (*bell*) over the nest to (*protect*) the lapwing and her (*babies*).

In the Roman Empire, being a Christian was hard because the Emperor wanted everyone to think he was the greatest!

After every mention of the animal, ask them to guess what it is!

Androcles, a Christian, was on his way to Rome when he stopped to help an animal in pain. The other travellers were in a hurry but Androcles said that no one should let animals suffer. He found something sharp in the poor creature's foot and easily pulled it out. The animal was relieved and seemed to smile.

In Rome, there was trouble for the Christians and the Emperor put some of them in prison. He felt like his favourite kind of live entertainment: Christians and animals in the circus ring together – hoping that each animal would kill a Christian!

Androcles was so scared he fell on his knees in the middle of the circus, closed his eyes and prayed for strength, hoping death would at least come quickly. When nothing happened, he opened his eyes and there to his astonishment was the animal he had helped on the way to Rome! It remembered Androcles and was so grateful that it couldn't bring itself to attack him. The crowds never got their entertainment and they hissed and booed!

Activities

Animals are an important feature of the natural world and feature in many traditional religious tales. The story-telling techniques used here may be interchanged quite easily.

Mime this story several times over and have the children add narrative and dialogue as they get into it.

The Prophet Muhammad is sitting on the ground in the courtyard of a mosque, discussing Muslim beliefs with a group of people. He is wearing a cloak which is spread out on the ground around him. A kitten wanders into the courtyard and sits down on the Prophet's cloak and falls asleep! When the Prophet is ready to go, he doesn't have the heart to disturb the kitten so he cuts round his cloak!

To read out or act

According to a Jewish legend, a very old woman was planting seeds at the edge of a wood, when a young man came along.

'Surely you don't think you'll live long enough to see those seeds grow into a tree, do you?' he asked.

'All these other trees,' she said, without looking up, 'were planted by people who lived before me and may have died without seeing the trees themselves. I'm planting this tree for those who will live after me even if I die without seeing it myself.'

Closing thoughts

Probably all the children will need some explanation of the pollutants mentioned, especially acid rain; but this adapted nursery rhyme will be all the more memorable:

Twinkle, Twinkle, Little Star

Twinkle, twinkle, little star,
How I wonder what you are.
Up above the world so high,
Like a diamond in the sky.

If the sky stays pure and clean,
We will see your twinkle bright.
But smoke, exhaust and acid rain
All will cloud your flickering light.

Twinkle, twinkle, little star.
I'd like to keep you as you are.

(Douglas W. Larche, *Father Gander Nursery Rhymes*, Advocacy Press, 1985, 0 911655 12 3, p. 42.)

Sayings from the Hadith, a collection of sayings which can be traced to the Prophet Muhammad:

If someone plants a tree and looks after it until it is fully grown and bears fruit, they will be rewarded by God.

If someone plants a tree or sows a field and people and animals can come and eat from it, it is as good as giving charity.

A saying of Rabindranath Tagore, an Indian poet, translated by Radha Krishnamoorti when she was 17. Ask the children to close their eyes and to visualise everything the reader mentions:

'Who do you worship in this lonely dark corner of the temple with all the doors shut? If you open your eyes, you will see that God is not in front of you. God is where the tiller is tilling the hard ground and where the stone-breaker is breaking hard stones. God is with them, come rain or shine.

'Take off your special cloak and, like God, come down to the dust. God is happy to join in the world and he is one of us forever.'

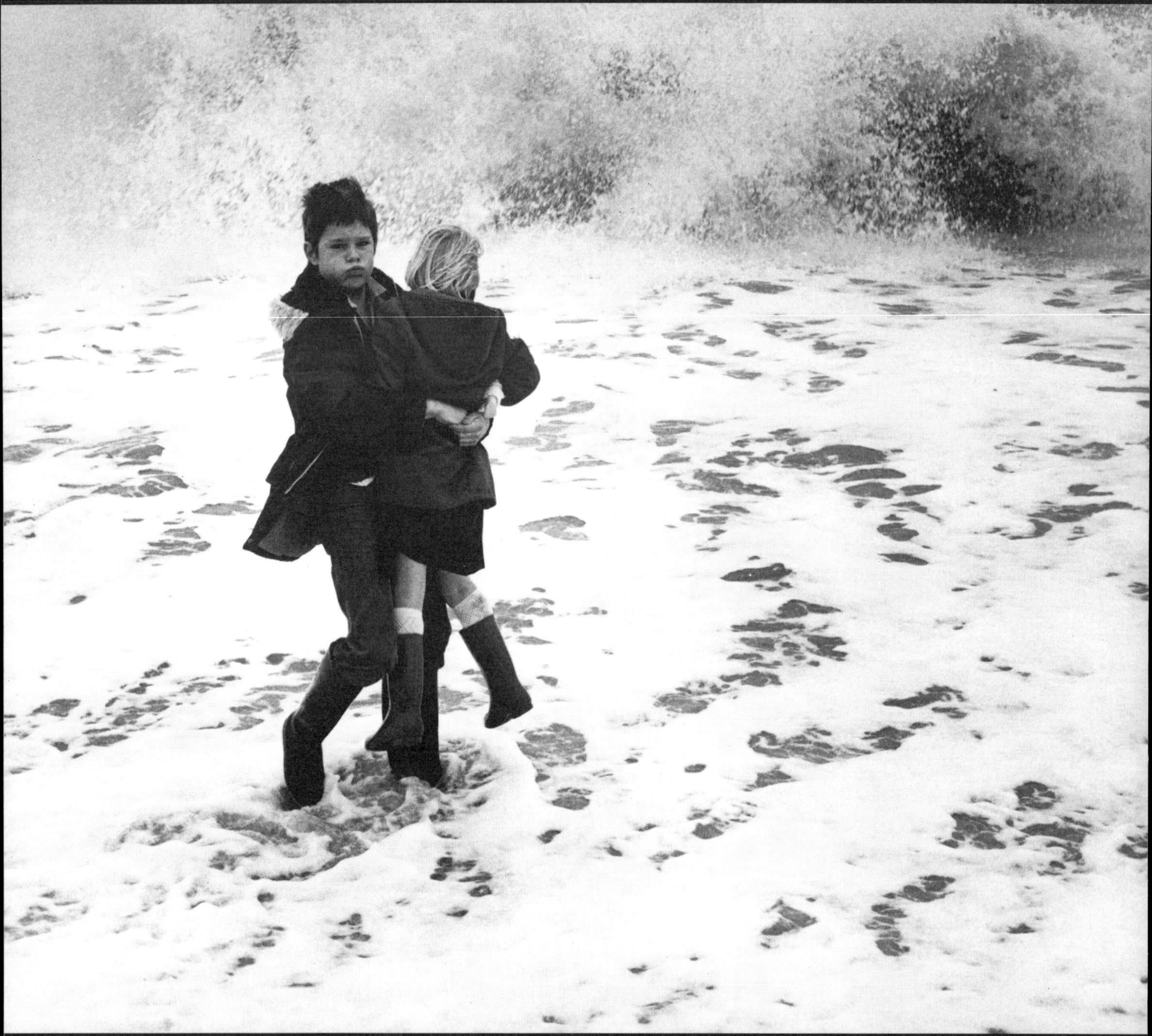

7

From me to you, with love

The need to give and receive love is so basic to human experience that it is little wonder that, in many world religions, relationships with other people are thought to be more like our relationship with God than anything else.

caring for other people

To read out

Living Death

There are poor people with nowhere to go,
No food, no family, no home.
Homeless people are human, too:
Their hearts can be broken like ours.
What will they do when it starts to rain?
How much more will they be hurt by pain?

Love has abandoned them
But loneliness will not leave them alone –
They have a living death.

(Raakhi Kanadia, age 14)

The video

It is vital to preview clip number 7 on the accompanying video cassette: some children may be distressed at the predicament of the homeless people portrayed; others may identify personally with them; yet others may have stereotypes which need to be addressed.

While homelessness is a broad concept covering those who live in temporary or unsuitable accommodation and while there may be a minority in any society who prefer to be rootless, the homeless in this clip are those who are forced to sleep literally on the city streets, longing for the security and dignity of their own home.

The 'Crisis at Christmas' charity is seen in action over a five-day holiday period: they serve food, distribute clothes and bedding and offer whatever comfort they can.

There are some people living in our cities who have no families to care for them and nowhere to live. They have to sleep on the cold streets at night and just eat whatever food people give them. You'll hear one man talking about his life: he has no job and no home to go to, and says it's not at all like the way he would really like to live.

Christmas is a happy time for Christians, and other people too, who enjoy being with their family, eating plenty of nice things, exchanging presents and having a lot of fun. A group of Christians, who feel it must be especially sad for people to be poor and lonely at Christmas, care so much that they give up time to be with the homeless. They serve them a hot meal, give them some warm clothes and talk to them like ordinary people, hoping that, at least for a short while, they will feel looked after and loved.

To read out

This is what some eight-year-olds said about helping homeless people:

Caring, caring,
Daring, daring,
Don't let me die!

I need water,
I need food,
Don't let me die!

I need a home,
I need a bed,
PLEASE don't let me die!

(Sam Blandy)

'When I was going to school, I saw a blind man and I helped him to cross the road, and I talked to him and he said he did not have a home and I looked after him.'   (Gurdarshin Khaira)

'If people need you, you must help them no matter what you have to do. Caring is when you give someone warmness.'
(Amanda Jayne Coker)

'If we don't care now, things will get worse.'   (Rami Cheblak)

'We need to love because it is bad for people to suffer.'
(Catherine Grigg)

'We need to help people because then they will be happy – and otherwise they might die!'   (Mumtaz Moledina)

Closing thoughts

This anonymous poem from Cuba may be used as a closing meditation: the need for openness to be shown by many people can be potently expressed by having the poem read more than once, in succession, each time by a different person, while everyone else has their eyes closed. This creates a 'voice over' effect.

My House

My house is not my house
If there's someone without a house
Alongside my house.

The thing is that my house
can't be my house
if it's not also the house
of whoever has no house.

(in Chris Searle (ed.), *Wheel around the world*, Macdonald, 1983, p. 32)

The poet, songwriter and singer Bob Marley, through whom perhaps more than anyone else Rastafarian culture was made widely known beyond the community, often took as his subject the need for warmth and kindness in a cold, cruel world. In these verses, he calls upon us all to unite ('inite') and love the whole human race ('Imanity') for God says ('Jah seh') that none of his children ('seeds') should be forsaken. The verses may be read with a rap beat and the children should be encouraged to clap lightly, sway in time or bounce rhythmically on their bottoms:

So Jah seh
Not one of my seeds
Shall sit in the sidewalk
and beg bread

And verily, verily
I'm saying unto thee
Inite oneself and love Imanity
Cause puss and dog get together
What's wrong with you my brother
So Jah seh.

(quoted in Henderson Dalrymple, *Bob Marley: Music Myth and the Rastas*, Carib-Arawak Publishing, 1976, p. 37)

Mix and match

Book box

Most primary schools abound with picture books and fiction on the subject of human relationships, but the following might be especially useful for this theme:

A series of books in which Nanette Newman has collected and arranged children's thoughts with some of their art; all are published by Collins: *God Bless Love*, 1972/6, 0 00 195280 3; *Vote for Love*, 1976, 0 00 183980 2; *Lots of Love*, 1974/7, 0 00 195288 9; *All Our Love*, 1978, 0 00 183752 4; *The Facts of Love*, 1980, 0 00 195292 7.

Robert Kraus, *Whose Mouse Are You?*, Picture Puffins, 1990, 0 14 050 092 8. An endearing monologue by a tiny mouse who expresses his devotion for his family.

Jenny Wagner, *John Brown, Rose and the Midnight Cat*, Picture Puffins, 1989, 0 14 050306 4. A story of insecurity, jealousy, resentment . . . and deep acceptance.

Elizabeth Sharma, *The Four Friends*, Tiger Books, 1985, 0 948137 150. A retelling, in several bilingual versions, of a tale from the Hindu classics.

Vera Gissing, *Samik and the Bear Child*, Macdonald, 1989, 0 356 16065 3. A delicately and authentically illustrated folk tale of the Inuit.

Yogesvara dasa and Jyotirmayi-devi dasi, *A Gift of Love: the story of Sudama the Brahmin*, Bala Books, 1982, 0 89647 015 6.

To read out

This passage of ten 'commandments' for friendship, written by a 15-year-old girl from Finland, works well if each couplet is read as a call and response by two people, taking a line each: that would involve twenty altogether. It may be wise sometimes to alter the gender of the 'friend', as appropriate:

If your friend is hungry or thirsty,

Give him your share.

If your friend is in want of love,

Love him.

If your friend is in want of home and clothes,

Give him a cottage and clothes.

If your friend is lonely,

Keep him company.

If your friend is lying,

Silence him.

If your friend calls to you,

Listen to him.

If your friend is laughing,

Laugh with him.

If your friend is crying,

Cry with him.

If your friend is ill,

Fetch help.

If your friend dies,

Don't forget him.

(Paula Lagerstam, in Richard and Helen Exley (eds), *Dear World*, Exley Publications, 1978, 0 905521 16 1, p. 111)

The song

A Dream of a Place

This song is based on the story of the same title in Angela Wood, *Faith Stories for Today*, BBC/Longman, 1990, 0 582 05946 1, pp. 4–9. In this traditional Jewish tale, the Temple is built on a place where great devotion was expressed, thus drawing prayer and love together.

The words and music were specially composed for *Assembly Kit* by Stephen Clark and the music was transcribed by Kate Buchanan.

With movement

1 Old Solomon had a problem: The Temple must be started right away. But where would be best For the Temple to rest? Yes, where should the people pray? 3 But Benjamin, he lived alone, He lived a quiet life. But Jonathan lived on the other side With his children and his loving wife.

D.C.

CODA (Ev'ry day), That's where the people pray.

2 Now there's a hill, a very proud hill,
　On Mount Moriah envy never shows,
　Where two brothers care
　And so everything's fair
　When they share what the harvest grows.

4 Then Benjamin thought of Jonathan,
　The children that his brother had to feed.
　It did not seem right
　So he planned late that night
　To answer his brother's need.

5 Then Jonathan thought of Benjamin,
　Of what a lonely life he must lead.
　It did not seem right
　So he planned late that night
　To answer his brother's need.

6 That night they took their sacks of food,
　And worked with loving care,
　But when they returned from each other's farms
　Yet another sack was sitting there.

7 And neither would have ever understood,
　Or ever learnt about the other's ploy,
　But dawn broke at last
　As the two brothers passed
　And they laughed till they cried with joy.

8 Old Solomon solved his problem,
　The Temple could be built without delay.
　If you look above
　On the Mountain of Love,
　Yes, that's where the people pray . . .

To read out

This Jewish folk-story is based on the idea that God's way of showing love for people is through *other* loving people.

- -

Once there was a terrible flood in a village and everybody ran for their life – everybody except one family who stayed inside their house. 'Come on, get in!' called their friends in a cart, as the water started to cover the street.

'No . . . we'll stay here: God will save us . . .'

'Hurry up, climb aboard!' called other friends, sailing by on a boat.

The waters rose over their heads and they felt themselves drowning.

'No . . . we'll stay here,' they replied from an upstairs window, 'God will save us.'

'Catch hold of this!' called some other friends, letting down a ladder from a helicopter.

'No . . . we'll stay here,' they answered from the roof. 'God will save us.'

'How could you do this to us!' they accused God. 'Why did you let us drown? Why didn't you save us?'

'But I tried,' God explained. 'I sent the cart, the boat and the helicopter!'

- -

To read out

'Love feels like a big heart bouncing inside me.
Love sounds like a heart bubbling up.
Love is the colour of red.
Love smells like a rose.'
(Robert Butler, age 8)

'Love feels like my heart beating.

Love sounds like butterflies flitting.

Love tastes of strawberry.'

(Michelle Devane, age 8)

Closing thoughts

This is particularly suitable for a going-home assembly or on any 'closing' occasion at which the children can reflect on what they have done. Four readers are best: one for each question and one for the beginning and end. Alternatively, children could prepare other questions which they think people could ask at the end of a day/week/term . . .

Many centuries ago, in China, there lived a very wise man called K'Ung Fu'Tzu; European and American people usually call him Confucius. K'Ung Fu'Tzu often gave advice to his friend Tseng Tzu and this is what he once said.

'Every night, I ask myself three things:

Did I do my best to help people?
Was I true and fair?
Have I only told others to do what I would do myself?

If so, I have been a good friend.'

The Gift of Friendship

Friendship is a priceless gift that can't be bought or sold;
And its value is far greater than a mountain made of gold.
For gold is cold and lifeless; it can neither see nor hear;
And in the time of trouble it is powerless to cheer.
It has no ears to listen, no heart to understand;
It cannot bring you comfort or reach out a helping hand.
So when you ask God for a gift, be thankful if he sends
Not diamonds, pearls or riches but the love of real true friends.

(a folk poem from Jamaica; origin unknown)

God bless all those that I love;
God bless all those that love me.
God bless all those that love those that I love
And all those that love those that love me.

(a prayer on an old sampler in New England; origin unknown)

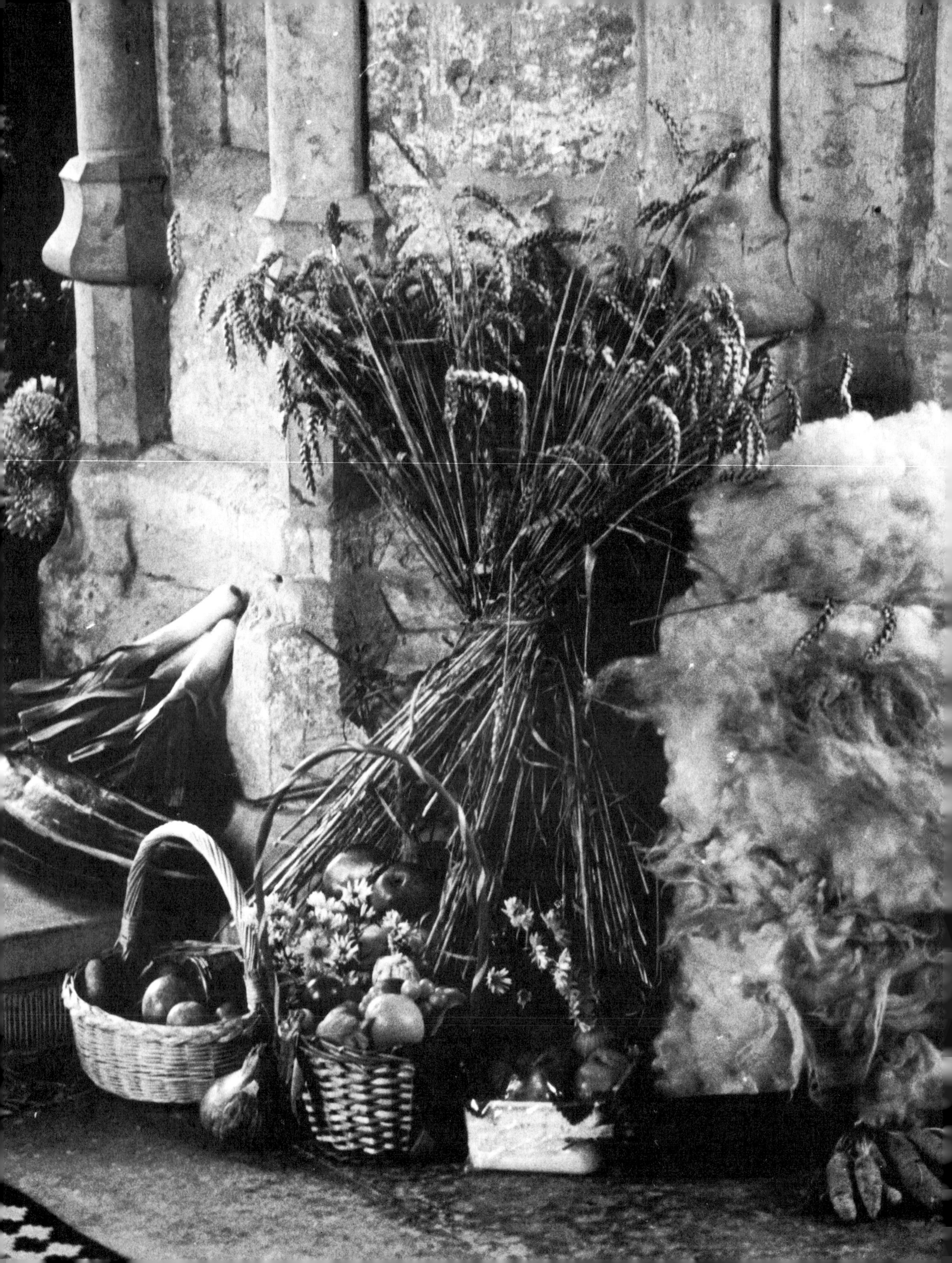

8

Yummy! I'm starving!

Food is one of life's great pleasures and many religious rituals involve the sharing of food – sometimes a kind of food which is only eaten to mark a special experience. The disciplines of fasting enable a reaching out to those who are starving or in need of the basic necessities of life. For most of the world, food is not fancy.

feasting, fasting and famine

An activity

The scene is breakfast; there should be a chair at a table on which the following are laid: cereal bowl, cup and saucer, plate, knife, fork, teaspoon, dessertspoon, tablespoon, cereal, teapot (with tea inside!), milk jug (with milk inside!), a slice of toast and a small saucepan containing baked beans.

Involve children beforehand in making a dummy newspaper with a bold front-page headline on the subject of world hunger.

The cast comprises the Head, or teacher, and six children, three of whom have light speaking parts: aim for a balance of gender in servers and speakers. The Head should discuss with them whether or not to say 'Thank you' when food is served and whether to comply, resist or be passive when food is removed.

The scene opens with the Head reading a newspaper at the table, taking care not to reveal the front-page headline.

Child 1 enters stage left, serves Head cereal with milk, and exits stage left.

Head takes a dessertspoonful of cereal and lifts it to lips but is prevented from eating by child 2 who enters stage right with a tray, snatches from the Head's hand the bowl and spoon and proclaims, 'Do you know how lucky you are to have wheat for breakfast? In some parts of the world, a bowlful of flour a day for a whole family is a luxury!' Child puts bowl and spoon and cereal packet on the tray and exits stage right.

Child 3 enters stage right, pours Head a cup of tea with milk and exits stage right.

Head stirs tea with teaspoon and lifts cup to lips but is prevented from drinking by child 4 who enters stage left with a tray, snatches from the Head's hand the cup, saucer and teaspoon and proclaims, 'Do you know how lucky you are to have tea and milk to drink? In some parts of the world, clean water is a real luxury!' Child puts cup, saucer, teaspoon, teapot and milk jug on the tray and exits stage left.

Child 5 enters stage left, puts a slice of toast on the breakfast plate, ladles a tablespoon of baked beans on to the toast, serves this to the Head and exits stage left.

Head cuts a bite-sized portion of beans on toast and lifts it to lips but is prevented from eating it by child 6 who enters stage right, snatches from the Head's hand the knife, fork and plate, and proclaims, 'Do you know how lucky you are to have beans on toast for breakfast? In some parts of the world, such a meal once a week is a real luxury!' Child puts knife, fork, plate, saucepan and tablespoon on tray and exits stage right.

The table is now empty, the Head looks up and down it to make the point, picks up the dummy newspaper and opens it out wide to reveal large front-page headline. The children involved may then come forward and declare the headline in a loud voice.

This drama/tableau may disturb some children who begin to see the implications world hunger may have for them. There should be ample opportunity for them to express how they feel and to discuss – perhaps beginning in situ and continuing in individual classrooms – some of the ways in which they might respond: adopting a simpler lifestyle; political action and representation, at the level they are able; charitable offerings and voluntary work; prayer and meditation . . .

To read out

The Inuit people live in the frozen north where it is too cold for plants to grow most of the year so they get their food by fishing and hunting. This poem is about the prayer of a young Inuit man who has not caught anything for a long time and is really hungry.

Hunger

Fear hung over me.
I dared not try
to hold out in my hut.

Hungry and chilled,
I stumbled inland,
tripping, falling constantly.

At Little Musk Ox Lake
the trout made fun of me;
they wouldn't bite.

On I crawled,
and reached the Young Man's River
where I had caught salmon once.

I prayed
for fish or reindeer
swimming in the lake.

My thought
reeled into nothingness
like run-out fishing line.

(in Chris Searle (ed.), *Wheel Around the World*, Macdonald, 1983, 0 356 09213 5, p. 46)

Closing thought

This is best read in a responsive fashion either by teacher and child or by two children per couplet and one child for each of the last three lines:

'God, when I am hungry
Give me someone to feed.

When I am thirsty
Give water for their thirst.

When I am sad,
Give me someone I can make happy.

When I am worried about myself,
Give me someone else to worry about.

God, when I want to be cared for,
Give me someone who really needs to be loved.

May what you want be bread for me to eat.
May your gentleness be my strength.
May your love be my resting-place.'

(from the French traditional prayer 'Prières pour une foi'; freely translated by Angela Wood)

Mix and match

An activity

For many children, harvest festivals at schools are quite incomprehensible because they follow the annual cycle and a year is too long a span of time for them to absorb. Additionally, children in urban environments, brought up on packaged food, have no experience of sowing, tending and reaping. Children in a rural setting may be more sensitive to growth and more aware of the natural processes involved in the food we eat, but nevertheless need opportunities to ritualise and symbolise their perceptions.

A 'quick' harvest festival can be developed within a classroom in which several kinds of edible shoots (various bean sprouts, mustard and cress) are grown. Try to stagger the planting by starting with the longest-growing and finishing with the shortest-growing, so that ideally the shoots will all be ready at about the same time. Children should be encouraged to communicate what they feel as the shoots are growing, through drama (especially if it can be recreated at the festival), art, music and any form of creative writing. On the day that the shoots will be 'harvested', there will be a festival in which the children will make sandwiches from their shoots and invite parents and other visitors to share in the thanksgiving for food. There they will recite and re-enact their creations and perhaps perform other pieces, such as traditional harvest songs and prayers or the 'Guinea Corn' poem in this section.

If possible buy or bake several kinds of bread and display them before making them into sandwiches: discuss with the children the various shapes, sizes, colours and textures of the bread and ask them to explore some of the ways in which bread is like people.

To read out

This anonymous poem from Jamaica is particularly effective when read as a call and response:

Guinea Corn

Guinea corn, I long to see you

Guinea corn, I long to plant you

Guinea corn, I long to mould you

Guinea corn, I long to weed you

Guinea corn, I long to hoe you

Guinea corn, I long to top you

Guinea corn, I long to cut you

Guinea corn, I long to dry you

Guinea corn, I long to beat you

Guinea corn, I long to trash you

Guinea corn, I long to parch you

Guinea corn, I long to grind you

Guinea corn, I long to turn you

Guinea corn, I long to eat you

(Chris Searle (ed.), *Wheel Around the World*, Macdonald, 1983, 0 356 09213 5, p. 43)

Book box

Sarah Hayes, *Eat Up, Gemma*, Walker, 1990, 0 7445 1328 6. A charming story about a black toddler who is a fussy and a messy eater.

John Burningham, *The Shopping Basket*, Picture Lions, 1980, 0 00 662148 1. A cumulative counting story involving a child.

John Vernon Lord with Janet Burroway, *The Giant Jam Sandwich*, Picture Piper, 1972/89, 0 330 30354 6. A story told in rhyming couplets of a desperate and 'food-based' attempt to rid a village of a gigantic swarm of wasps.

June Jones, *Ramadan and Eid-ul-Fitr*, Blackie, 1986, 0 216 91987 8. A reader in the 'Citylinks' series about the Muslim month of fasting and the festival of celebration which follows.

Floella Benjamin, *Exploring Caribbean Food in Britain*, 0 947679 898, and Shahrukh Husain, *Exploring Indian Food in Britain*, 0 947679 901; both Mantra Publishing, 1988. A group of children shop and cook a range of food, learning about the origin of the ingredients and the significance of the dishes.

Angela Wood, 'What It's Worth', in *Faith Stories for Today*, BBC/Longman, 1990, 0 582 05946. A traditional Muslim tale based on a historical figure.

The song

The Lord Made the Apple

Samira Habashi has taught this Arabic song to many children and they all love it! The words are taken from a collection of verses and short stories published in Cairo under the title *Kitab al Muslim Asarir* (meaning *A Book for Young Muslims*). Samira composed the music and it was transcribed by Walter Robson. The simple English version was written by Angela Wood.

With movement

Look here! Look here! See the ap-ple! Look here! Look here! See the ap-ple!
On-thurr, On-thurr, lil-too-fa-ha! On-thurr, On-thurr, lil-too-fa-ha!

Who made it so red? Who made it so big? Who made it so sweet?
Man ham-arr-ha? Man kab-barr-ha? Man ha'-al'-ha?

Yum-my! Yum-my! Yum-my! Yum! Who made it so round? The Lord, the Great
Yum-my! Yum-my! Yum-my! Yum! Man ka-warr-ha? Al-lah hu ta-

One, The Lord, who made all! The Lord, the Great One, The Lord, who made all!
hal! All'-hall'-a-lak! Al-lah hu ta-hal! All'-hall'-a-lak!

74

An activity

Jeanne Willis, *The Tale of Mucky Mabel*, Beaver Books, 1986, 0 09 939820 6. A cautionary tale in rhyming couplets about a girl with disgusting eating habits who is one day picked up by a farmer, mistaking her for a pig who meanwhile is having lunch with Mabel's parents! They are delighted that 'Mabel' said grace before she ate and is using a serviette.

The story raises important questions for children about the role of food in civilised behaviour, the humanising effects of eating with others and the idea of thanks and praise for the gift of food. Several situation dramas are easy to create and serve to sharpen up these issues:

- Create a scene in which the person who receives one of Mabel's peas in their eye complains to the restaurateur. What attitude do Mabel's parents (and others) adopt? How is the matter resolved?

- Mabel's eating habits put her parents off their food. Imagine that Mabel's parents go to the doctor and explain why they are not eating enough. The doctor wants to see Mabel as well! What treatment does the doctor recommend for the parents? Do they accept that?

- What does the pig say as 'Grace' before meals?

- A situation might develop in which Mabel was having school dinners and the kitchen staff refused to serve her as she showed no respect for the food they had prepared! What action does the Head take? How do other children react?

- The story can be extended to the pigsty where Mabel arrives in the farmer's sack. She protests that she is not a pig but a person. Several children might suggest – and enact – what is essentially human that Mabel is able to do or be . . .

The video

Clip number 8 on the accompanying video cassette shows three examples of food used in religious celebration or gatherings and the children may need to deal with them one at a time (see notes on clip number 1 on page 18 for this method).

Something that makes humans different is that they are the *only* beings that *cook* food. Most people eat every day but at special times there are special dishes – and often lots of them! You will see people cooking and eating festival food.

A Jewish woman is frying latkes. She made a mixture of grated potato and onion and then spooned it into sizzling oil in the frying pan. It is the festival of Hanukah and the family will enjoy the latkes when they have lit their Hanukah candles.

A gurdwara is a place where Sikhs meet to pray, to read their holy book, to learn all sorts of things and just to spend time together and welcome guests. An important part of the gurdwara is the langar which is a big kitchen. Sikhs bring food to cook and share and anyone – whoever they are – can eat there.

Children in a church school have been making a cake for their Christmas party. When they are sitting down, enjoying themselves, Father Christmas arrives and samples their cake!

The cassette

'Giving' is a heart-warming and inspiring story on the accompanying audio cassette, which concerns an African family in a famine-stricken area. The two children befriend two others who have been orphaned and secretly share with them some of their food. Their parents discover this and try to be cross but their humour and humanity are too strong!

To read out

Roberta, Peter and Phyllis lived in a town but when their father was suddenly taken away they had to move to the country. They knew he was in trouble because of what he said or wrote but they did not really understand what was going on. It was dark when they got to their new home and they were cold, tired and hungry but their mother had sent some money to a woman in the village, asking her to get some food in and lay it out in the dining-room. There was no electricity in those days so they tried to find their way round by the light of a candle.

. . . .

The dining-room opened out of the kitchen . . . There was a table certainly, and there were chairs, but there was no supper. 'Let's look in the other rooms,' said Mother; and they looked . . . but there was nothing to eat . . . 'What a horrid old woman!' said Mother, 'she's just walked off with the money and not got us anything to eat at all.'

'Then shan't we have any supper at all?' asked Phyllis, dismayed . . .

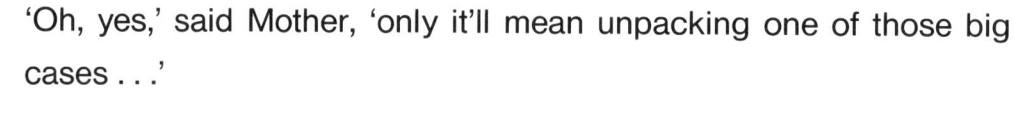

'Oh, yes,' said Mother, 'only it'll mean unpacking one of those big cases . . .'

'Hooray!' said Mother, 'here are some candles – the very first thing! You girls go and light them . . .'

When the cloth was spread on the table, a real feast was laid out on it. Everyone was very, very tired, but everyone cheered up at the sight of the funny and delightful supper. There were biscuits, the Marie and the plain kind, sardines, preserved ginger, cooking raisins, and candied peel and marmalade . . . ●

Next morning Roberta woke Phyllis by pulling her hair gently, but quite enough for her purpose. 'Wassermarrer?' asked Phyllis, still almost wholly asleep.

'... We'll just creep down mouse-quietly, and have everything beautiful before Mother gets up. I've woken Peter. He'll be dressed as soon as we are.' They had made an excellent fire, and had set the kettle on it at about half past five. So that by eight the fire had been out for some time, the water had all boiled away, and the bottom was all burned out of the kettle ...

'... I've found another room' (said Mother), 'I'd quite forgotten there was one. And it's magic! And I've boiled the water for tea in a saucepan.'

The forgotten room opened out of the kitchen. In the agitation and half darkness the night before its door had been mistaken for a cupboard's. It was a little square room, and on its table, all nicely set out, was a joint of cold roast beef, with bread and butter, cheese, and a pie.

(Edith Nesbit, *The Railway Children*, Magnet, 1906/1988, 0 416 11992 1, pp. 27–34.)

Closing thought

I'd Like to Squeeze

I'd like to squeeze this round world
into a new shape

I'd like to squeeze this round world
like a tube of toothpaste

I'd like to squeeze this round world
fair and square

I'd like to squeeze it and squeeze it
till everybody had an equal share

(John Agard in Morag Styles (ed.), *You'll Love This Stuff!*, Cambridge University Press, 1989, 0 521 31275 2, p. 41)

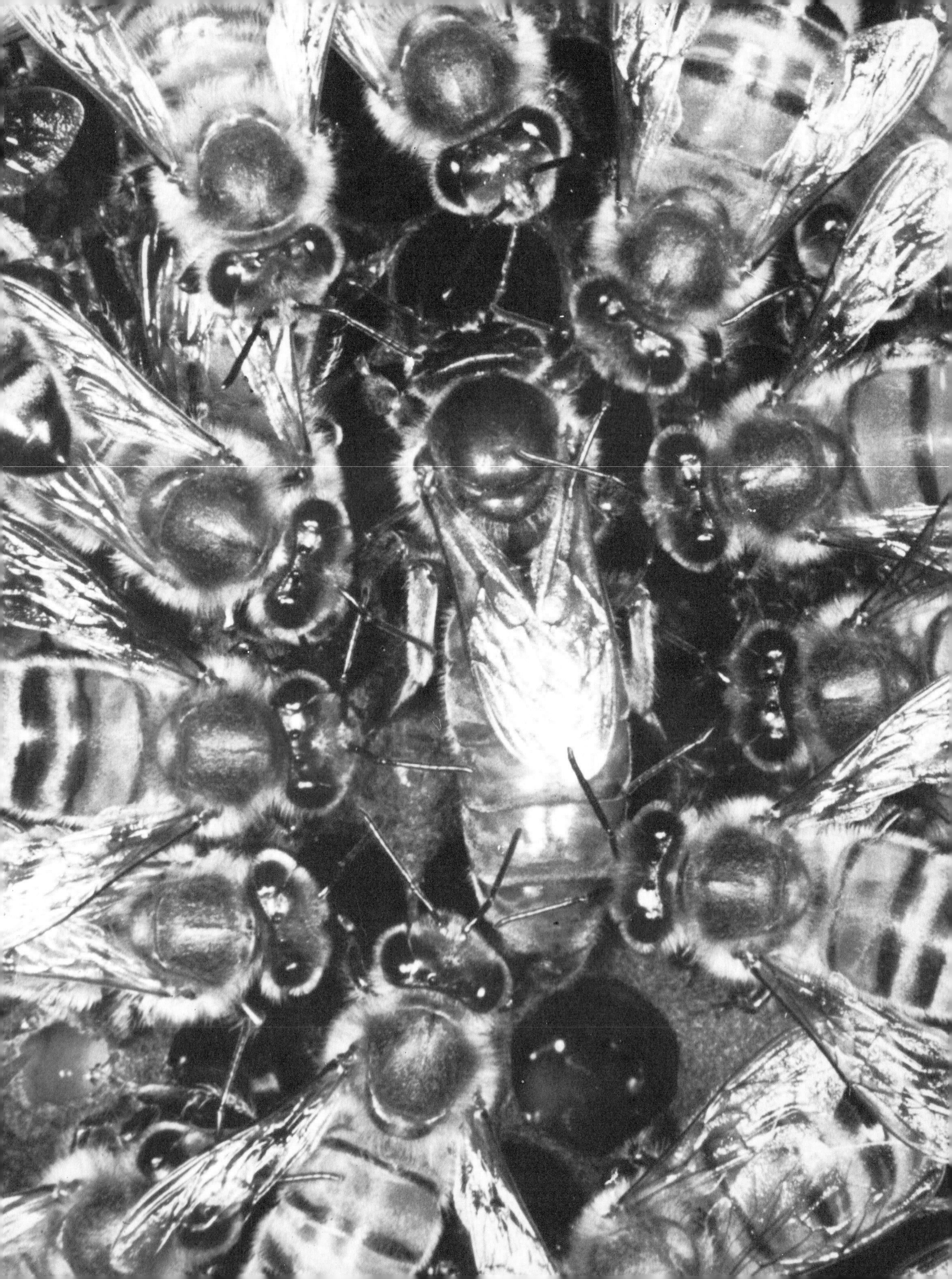

9 All together now!

The whole is more than the sum of its parts and together individuals can accomplish what they could not even consider alone. In some traditions, belonging to a community – and being fully individual within it – is thought to be the ideal way of life and all religions promote a sense of responsibility to society and a sense of the unity of the human race.

cooperation and community spirit

The video

The news item, which comprises clip number 9 on the accompanying video cassette, concerns the desperate international attempt in October 1988 to rescue three grey whales trapped in frozen Arctic waters. The commentary refers to 'eskimos' but this term is now discredited as a quite offensive nickname. They call themselves 'Inuit' which literally means 'people'. *Caution the children not to try and hold their breath as long as whales.*

Whales are big animals that live in the sea. Like us, they cannot breathe under water and they have to keep coming up for air every 20 or 30 minutes: that's about as long as play-time after dinner. The whales in our story spend the summer in the cool water quite near the North Pole and when winter comes they swim south to warmer places. One year it was still quite warm in the autumn but winter came suddenly. Most of the whales left quickly but three of them didn't realise in time and the water started to freeze and they got left behind.

Some Inuit people on the land nearby noticed the poor whales and bored through the ice to give them air-holes: that saved them for the time being. Soon people from America and Russia arrived with mechanical diggers and ice-breaking ships. They made a lot of noise and probably frightened the whales but they did make a clear way to the open sea where the whales could be free and safe. The two big whales swam off to find their friends but we don't know what happened to the tiny one. The Russians and Americans had not been very friendly to each other before but they worked together to break the ice and the two countries are much friendlier now since they helped the whales.

The language of the commentary is at quite a high register and may be difficult for young children to follow. Once or twice the blinding whiteness of the snow makes it hard for them to discern whales and rescuers. Familiarising the children with the story and supplying them with simple technical information, therefore, will increase their powers of observation and heighten their appreciation of the event. Extremely helpful is a simple book, illustrated with black and white drawings, chronicling the story: Giles Whittell, *The Story of Three Whales*, Telegraph Books/Walker Books, 1988, 0 74451 367 7.

To read out

Boundaries Down

It was cold and it was wet
And we never should forget
For we wouldn't want to see it happen twice.
It was all about the whales
And the night we bit our nails
When we found them trapped beneath the winter ice.

It surprises everyone
For the Gray Whales should be gone
Not struggling here so far from open sea.
So in all the snow and sleet
We had challenges to meet
Of how to set the lonely Gray Whales free.

So the people tried with blades
And with axes, picks and spades
But the ice was getting thicker by the day.
It was all that they could do,
Cutting holes for breathing through,
Let alone to help the Gray Whales get away.

Then the news began to spread
That the whales would soon be dead
And the world decided something must be done.
So the might of U.S.A.
And the Russians made their way
And they met on ice, beneath the Arctic sun.

▶

Now the old ways were to change
There's a world to rearrange
As these two brave countries fought the winter gales.
For instead of threats of war
Like we'd always seen before
They began to work together for the whales.

And the whole world held its gaze
On those cold and savage days
As we watched the superpowers work as one.
With the lucky whales' release
Then we saw a glimpse of peace,
Just as if the fear of fighting now was gone.

We saw boundaries down,
Promises made,
Friendships built,
Foundations laid.
And people all around the world
Showed that they care about
Two Gray Whales
Swimming out there . . .

(specially written for *Assembly Kit* by Stephen Clark)

Closing thought

Hug O' War

I will not play at tug o' war.
I'd rather play at hug o' war.
Where everyone hugs
Instead of tugs,
Where everyone giggles
And rolls on the rug,
Where everyone kisses,
And everyone grins,
And everyone cuddles,
And everyone wins.

(Shel Silverstein, *Where the Sidewalk Ends*, Harper and Row, 1974, p. 19.)

Mix and match

To read out

This might be even more meaningful for the children if the name of the school or the community is substituted for 'Suriname':

One Tree

one tree
so many leaves
one tree

one river
so many creeks
all are going to one sea

one head
so many thoughts
thoughts among which one good one
must be

one god
so many ways of worshipping
but one father

one Suriname
so many hair types
so many skin colours
so many tongues
one people

(Dobru Ravales in Chris Searle (ed.), *Wheel Around the World*, Macdonald, 1983, 0 356 09213 5, p. 55)

To read out

I Corinthians 12: 14–26 is about the community, using the image of the body composed of interdependent parts. Though much of the passage is difficult, if paraphrased it is quite easy for even young children to understand.

Book box

Robert Kraus, *Come Out and Play, Little Mouse*, Walker Books, 1990, 0 7445 1470 3. A little mouse is rescued by his brother disguised as a dog.

Pat Hutchins, *Tom and Sam*, Picture Puffins, 1981, 0 14 050 042 1. Tom and Sam were best friends until jealousy crept in.

Anthony Browne, *A Walk in the Park*, Picturemac, 1986, 0 333 41688 0. Two families represent different social classes symbolised by the distance that Mr Smith and Mrs Smythe keep between them.

Win Morgan, *Kippy Koala and the Bushfire*, Lion, 1985, 0 85648 892 5. Aspects of this book will terrify the very young or the delicate; the koala cannot run fast and, when the bush catches fire, has to ride on the kangaroo's back!

Leo Lionni, *It's Mine!*, Picture Knight, 1989, 0 340 50709 8. A toad complains to the young frogs that they are always fighting and shouting, 'It's mine!' about everything.

Tony Johnston, *The Quilt Story*, Macdonald, 1988, 0 356 16055 6. The quilt Abigail's mother makes for her becomes a part of her life.

Carol Purdy, *Iva Dunnit and the Big Wind*, Beaver Books, 1989, 0 09 959590 7. Set in the 'pioneering' days of American history, this story concerns an intrepid woman who prides herself that her children 'stay put'.

Madhur Jaffrey, 'The Mango Tree', in *Seasons of Splendour*, Puffin Books, 1987, 0 14 031854 2, pp. 94f.

Kiri Te Kanawa, 'The Trees of the Forest', in *Land of the Long White Cloud*, Pavilion Books, 1989, 1 85145 176 5, p. 83. A traditional Maori tale in which an arrogant tree is put in its place, indistinguishable from all the others.

Michael Foreman, *War and Peas*, Picture Puffins, 1974/87, 0 14 050243 2. Famine in the land makes King Lion and the Minister for Food, a grocer, visit the neighbouring country to ask for a little of their surplus food. A battle ensues and the fat king asks for the recipe for peace!

To read out

Familiarise the children with the standard format and they can create recipes. This is created by Ester Gluck, age 7:

Recipe for Peace

Ingredients:

friendship, love, understanding, caring and none of their opposites.

Method:

You put the friendship and love in your heart. When they go down, the understanding and caring goes into your thoughts. When the person has finished talking about their problems – and that person can be anybody – try very hard not to have enemies. When it's ready, you give everybody a bit and they all have peace. When I said everybody, I mean everybody in the world. When you eat it, don't bring it up again!

To read out or act

An elderly woman lives with her married daughter's family and, as she gets older, she shakes when she eats and spills her food. Her daughter and son-in-law get her a wooden bowl and spoon and sit her in the corner on the floor at mealtimes. One day, they notice the children carving a piece of wood and ask what it is. The children reply that they are making a trough for them, their parents, to eat from when they get old.

What do you think the parents do?

(In this story of unknown source, the parents see through the children's activity that they too are vulnerable and dependent on others; they are filled with remorse and return the elderly mother to a place of honour in the family. If the story has been acted out rather than told, the children might present their suggestions for the parents' behaviour in role.)

The song

Allah, There's Only One God!

The Arabic line in this song is the Muslim statement of faith, the 'Shahadah' – 'There is no God but Allah . . .' This is the final part of a song composed by Yusuf Islam and has been transcribed by Walter Robson. The transliteration of the Arabic line is by Angela Wood.

1-5 Al - lah, there's only one God, {and Muhammad is / and Jesus was / and Moses was / and Abraham was / and Noah was} his messenger! Al - lah, *la ee-la-ha ee-lal la.

Al - lah, there's only one God and he created Adam And we are the children of Adam. Al - lah, la ee-la-ha ee-lal la.

* Elide the two vowels, sounding almost as 'lye'.

To read out or act

With the minimum of costume, this story, which is of uncertain origin, can be enacted simply yet boldly: there are five parts.

A tree had glossy leaves, a strong trunk and deep roots, and bore sweet fruit. The parts all lived happily together, sharing in the life of the whole tree, until one day each part began to feel more important than the others and they began to quarrel.

Trunk said, 'I am the most important because I stand tall and straight, my bark keeps us all safe and whenever people attack the tree, it's always me that gets it!'

Roots replied, 'Even if you can't see us, we're deep in the ground, holding you up! Where would you be without us, Trunk? You'd fall over, that's what!'

Leaves added, 'You're not the only ones that look after the whole tree, Trunk and Roots! What do you think we do? We keep the hottest sun rays and the heaviest rain from getting to you. You never burned up, did you? And you never got drenched? Well, you've got us to thank for that!'

Then Fruit joined in, 'We are juicy and delicious and it's because of us that there is a Tree at all. If it wasn't for us, there wouldn't be any of you!'

Finally Tree had something to say: what do you think it was?

(Children may have a range of suggestions; the story's 'answer' is that all the parts of the tree are important and connected. Without any one of them, the tree would not be a tree!)

Closing thought

This Mozambique poem begs to be recited in a circle of hands!

The Wheel Around the World

If all the world's children
wanted to play holding hands
they could happily make
a wheel around the sea.

If all the world's children
wanted to play holding hands
they could be sailors
and build a bridge across the seas.

What a beautiful chorus we would make
singing around the earth
if all the humans in the world
wanted to dance holding hands!

('Children's Song' in Chris Searle (ed.), *Wheel Around the World*, Macdonald, 1983, 0 356 09213 5, p. 50)

For greatest impact, have each couplet read respectively by a man; a woman; and a pair/group of children.

There is only one man in the world
and his name is All Men.
There is only one woman in the world
and her name is All Women.
There is only one child in the world
and the child's name is All Children.

(Carl Sandburg in 'Prologue' to *The Family of Man*, New York Museum of Modern Art, 1955, p. 3)

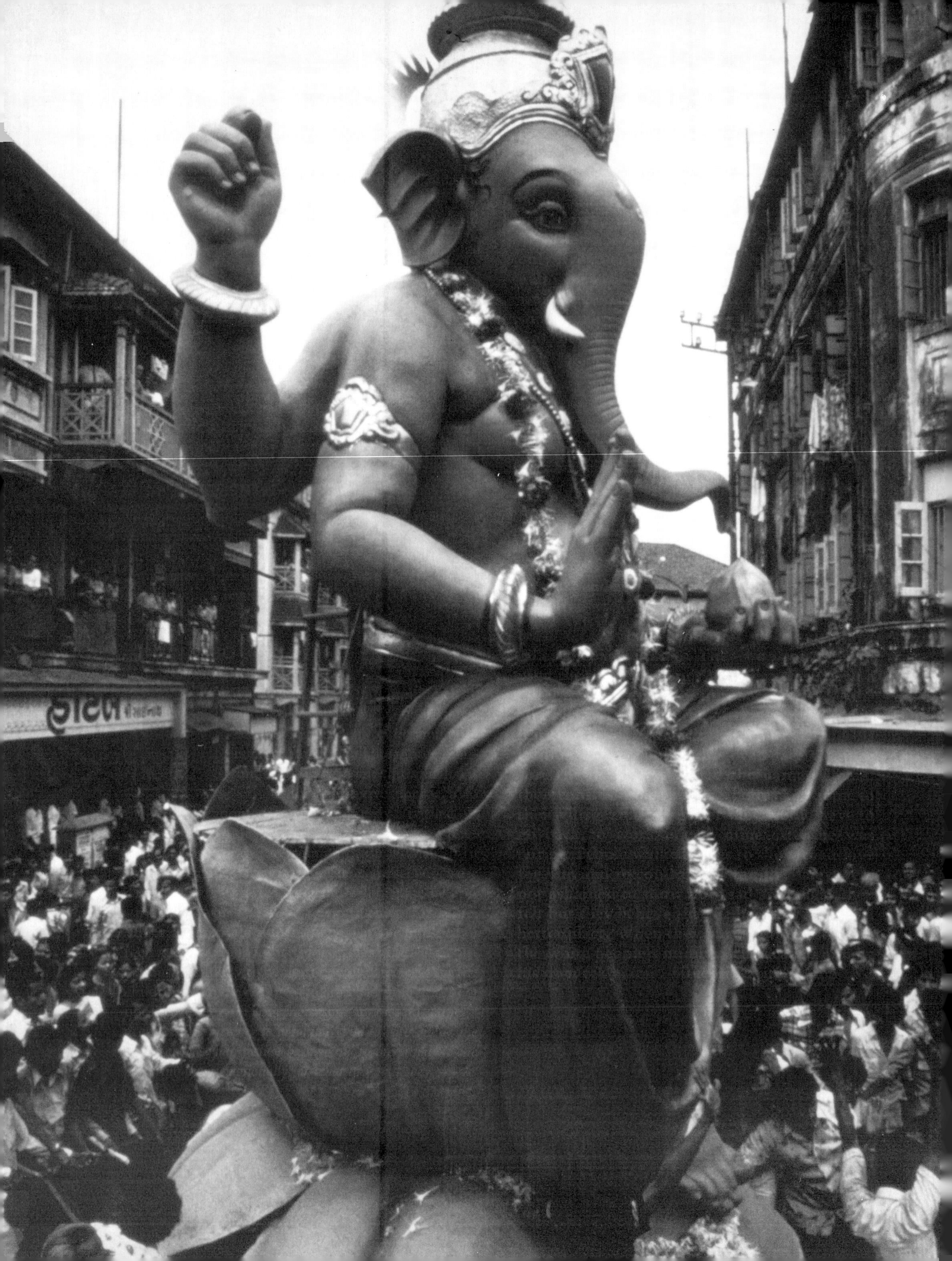

10

Fair's fair

The belief that we are all different yet equal is a strand running through many of the world's religious traditions. Yet this principle is seldom practised and the world we know is very unequal. Children's natural sense of justice is both outraged and overwhelmed by this and they need concrete examples, positive support and attractive role models to change things for the better.

justice and equality

To read out

Have you ever had so much to eat that you feel if you had another single bite, you'd absolutely explode? Then someone offers you something really tasty – your absolutely favourite food – and you say to yourself, 'I could probably manage just a mouthful . . . I'm sure I have room for a tiny bite . . .'?

These two stories – the first Jewish and the second Sikh – though separated by centuries and continents, are extraordinarily similar. They declare that room can always be made for something that is really needed.

• •

There were so many people praying in the synagogue that the place was absolutely packed and no one could move. Every seat was taken, people were standing in the aisles, sitting on the steps and perching on each other's knees. In fact they joked that if they had needed another sheet of paper in their prayer book, they could not have fitted it in! Even outside, there were crowds round the door and faces peering in through the windows. Suddenly, someone saw the Rabbi coming down the street and called in, 'The Rabbi's coming! There's going to be a special talk!' Without a single push or shove, everyone inside stepped back: extra space seemed to come from nowhere and they easily cleared a way for the Rabbi to pass!

• •

Guru Nanak and his friend, Mardana, had been on the road for days and had nearly reached the town of Multan. It was famous because people came from miles around to ask for help from its priests and religious teachers. Some of them saw the two travellers trudging along the dusty road up to the city gates and they became very jealous. 'We don't want them here,' they said. 'People will turn to them for help – and then where will we be?'

'But we can't say that to them, can we?' others replied. So they thought of a plan to make Guru Nanak go away, by dropping a hint that the town was simply too full! They carefully filled a bowl with milk right up to the brim and gave it to a messenger with the order, 'Go and meet them and hand them this bowl of milk. Keep it absolutely flat and carry it very slowly – mind you don't spill a single drop!' ●

The bowl of milk was very tempting: it looked lovely and cool and they were hot, tired and thirsty. But Guru Nanak knew it was not for drinking; in fact he understood completely what the people who sent it were trying to say: just as there is no room for another drop of milk in the bowl, so there is no room for another teacher in the city! But he had a sign for them, too. 'Hold it still, please,' he asked the messenger. Then he plucked a tiny jasmine blossom that was growing nearby and gently dropped it on to the surface of the milk: it was so light and fragile that it floated on the milk without making it tip over and its delicate fragrance scented all the milk. 'Please take that back to the people who sent you,' Guru Nanak said to the messenger, 'and explain to them that there is always room for holiness and goodness in the world.'

Minutes later, the priests and teachers themselves rushed to welcome Guru Nanak and Mardana into their city!

Closing thought

This would be an opportunity to mention some of the things which trouble children and which they would like to change:

There are many things wrong with our world that we could put right; there are lonely children that we could make our friends . . .

We can make room in our lives for them; room in our thoughts; room in our hearts; room in our prayers . . .

Mix and match

Book box

Babette Cole, *King Change-a-lot*, Picture Lions, 1988, 0 00 663 151 7. An alternative fairy tale in which a baby prince reforms the corrupt realm his parents have created.

Martin Baynton, *Jane and the Dragon*, Sainsbury's/Walker Books, 1988, 0 7445 1050 3. Jane cannot fulfil her ambition to be a knight because she is a girl . . .

Anthony Browne, *Bear Goes to Town*, Beaver Books, 1987, 0 09 932040 1. With his magic pencil, Bear is able to draw reality into any situation.

Sheila Segal, *Joshua's Dream*, Union of American Hebrew Congregations, 1985, 0 8074 0272 9. A touching story, told as though a Jewish parent and child were sitting round a family album.

Ingri and Edgar Parin D'Aulaire, *Pocahontas*, Doubleday, 1989, 0 385 26607 3. Now a heroine of North American history, this Amerindian girl played a vital role in the Jamestown settlement.

Nigel Gray, *A Country Far Away*, Puffin Books, 1990, 0 14 050954 2. The emotional experiences of a child in an industrialised society and a child in a developing society run parallel, though the conditions of their lives are vastly different.

Early Times ('The independent newspaper for young people'), published weekly by Garth Publications Ltd, Brighton Business Centre, 95 Ditchling Road, Brighton BN1 4SE, and available from local newsagents. Many events pose moral questions which might inform and inspire collective worship.

The cassette

In the story 'Alison and the Bike' on the accompanying audio cassette, Alison is suffering from divided loyalties and is caught in a moral dilemma because she has made two conflicting promises. She talks her problem through with her mother who is sympathetic and concerned that Alison do the right thing but refuses to decide the issue for her and says she must make up her own mind.

An activity

A cheer-leader or chorus-line style is an effective way to communicate this acrostic. You will need twenty children and twenty pieces of card (e.g. A4 size). Boldly write each of the twenty initials (S, T, A, N, D etc.) on a piece of card and give it to a child to hold in both hands. Arrange these children in the order of the acrostic, allowing for the spaces between words, so that it will read correctly from left to right from the point of view of the assembled gathering. They should then crouch down until their moment comes – that is, they should leap up and reveal their initial (either at chest level or above the head, as agreed) when the relevant line of the acrostic is read out. If all goes to plan, by the time the acrostic has been read, the title is as large as life! Then ask the whole of the assembled gathering to stand up and declare the statement as proudly as they can.

To read out

Stand Up For Your Rights

Sometimes things go wrong,
Terribly wrong,
And what can you do?
Never give up!
Do something!

Unbelievable things happen!
Please stand up for me!

For I am scared,
Oh please,
Really I am!

You've got to help!
Or at least get someone else to.
Utter nonsense, you may say!
Release me from this pain.

Righteousness –
I know we will win.
Goodness me, I didn't know it would come to this.
Help!
Till this is over I will never sleep.
Still, we will win yet.

(Susan Umpleby, age 11)

The song

What It's worth

This song is based on the story of the same title by Angela Wood, *Faith Stories for Today*, BBC/Longman, 1990, 0 582 05946 1, pp. 40–5. In this Muslim tale set in time of famine, Umar, the fourth caliph, ignores the needs of the wealthy, who can take care of themselves, and serves the poor. Rich is the reward!

The words and music were especially written for *Assembly Kit* by Stephen Clark and the music was transcribed by Kate Buchanan.

Apart from the piano/guitar accompaniment, some simple percussion, a flute, recorder or tuned percussion instrument (such as glockenspiel) would be very effective, playing improvised 'fills' around the scale of G minor around the song.

2 The months went by and the sun shone down
   The fire that never stops.
   Medina was a beautiful town
   Until they lost their crops.
   And Medina prayed for rain
   But Medina prayed in vain;
   For nothing ever comes to people who never
      learn
   That nothing ever comes until you wait your
      turn.

4 Then one day as the sun shone down
   A girl leapt to her feet.
   She saw a vision close to the town
   Of things to drink and eat.
   And she cried out to her friend
   The pain would surely end;
   But nothing ever comes to people who never
      learn
   That nothing ever comes until you wait your
      turn.

5 The people gathered all around
   To greet the man who came –
   His camel laden to the ground –
   The rich folk had no shame.
   And they offered him a price
   To sell his merchandise;
   But nothing ever comes to people who never
      learn
   That nothing ever comes until you wait your
      turn.

6 The first one offered all he had
   And the next one offered more.
   The price went up and still they fought
   For the food they were craving for.
   And the last man offered seven times
   What the food was really worth.
   But the man said 'no' and the rich folk found
   That money can't buy the earth.

7 The man rode on and the sun shone down
   He reached the poorer folk.
   They couldn't believe their hungry eyes
   And then the kind man spoke,
   'As you never lived by greed
   Just take ev'rything you need';
   For nothing ever comes to people who never
      learn
   That nothing ever comes until you wait your
      turn.

8 The months went by and the sun shone down,
   It left Medina dry.
   Medina was a beautiful town
   Beneath a cloudless sky.
   On the dry and dusty plain
   The rich folk prayed for rain;
   But nothing ever comes to people who never
      learn
   That nothing ever comes until you wait your
      turn.
   But nothing ever comes to people who never
      learn
   That nothing ever comes until you wait your
      turn.

With movement

1. The months went by and the sun shone down It left Medina dry.
Medina was a beautiful town Beneath a cloudless sky.
On the dry and dusty plain The people prayed for rain;
But nothing ever comes to people who never learn
That nothing ever comes until you wait your turn.

Slower

3. At first it was the poor people, Like it's always been since then, Who had no food, who had no hope, Who begged from the wealthy men. But time wore on and the rich folk found, Like the poor people found first, If the well is dry and the shelves are bare Then money doesn't quench your thirst.

D.C.

An activity

'The universe is built on three things: justice, truth and peace.'

This traditional Jewish saying, attributed to Rabban ben Gamliel and dating from ancient times, might be recited at any assembly on this theme. It would also serve well as a banner or even as a simple piece of sculpture. Arrange three large wooden stage/gymnastics blocks in a prominent position. Label them JUSTICE (or 'being fair'), TRUTH (or 'telling the truth') and PEACE (or 'making peace') respectively and/or hang on the side facing the front a child's work of art depicting the concept and/or group on the top of the blocks certain items which children and teachers consider symbolise the concepts (e.g. scales, tape recorder, flowers).

Groups of children might be invited to prepare a simple piece of drama or mime on one, two or all three of the concepts and perform it around the appropriate block, perhaps involving some of the objects which have been placed on top.

The video

The news report, in clip number 10 on the accompanying video cassette, is a moving account of a community in mourning. It is all the more poignant for the racist context in which it is set and the insensitive approach to the tragedy adopted by the oppressive regime. It bears witness to the struggle for dignity and is a phenomenal tribute to the triumph of the human spirit amid the anguish of suffering. There are scenes of the dead and bereaved, for which all will need to be prepared and which may be too disturbing for some. Older children and adults, enraged by the injustice of the experience and aware of its wider political implications, are likely to be most deeply affected. Yet the children who viewed the clip, and had time to reflect upon it alone and together, remember and value it greatly. *Pre-viewing is absolutely vital as are giving the pupils an adequate factual background to the situation and preparing them emotionally for what they will see.*

Most people in South Africa are black but the white people get most of the money and have a lot of power. There are laws to stop black people doing lots of things that white people are allowed to do and white people get a lot more chances than blacks. Black people can only live in certain places where there are not many jobs so the men must go far away to get work and are only allowed to come home for a short while each year. They miss their families and their families miss them, and the women have to look after everything while the men are away.

Underground there is gold and precious stones, and companies owned by white people have built mines to bring the minerals up so that they can be sold. Most people who go down the mines are black and the work is very dusty, dark and dangerous. Because the ground is hard, the miners have to blow up part of the rock to make a way through. The greedy companies make the miners work too fast and don't spend enough to keep them safe: there are often accidents and people get killed.

In 1986, a terrible explosion in a gold mine killed six black miners. The white bosses never used the miners' names but gave them each a number: they wrote the numbers on the coffins and piled them up. One of them was Simeon Katiti Sambo, who was 25 years old, and his brother had to look at his dead face to make sure the number matched the name. He and their cousins took Simeon's body back home to their village, knowing that they would have to go back to work in the mine after he was buried. People walked miles to show their love for him and to comfort his family. They were not ashamed to show how sad and angry they felt but they believe that he has now gone to a better place. When they buried him, instead of the white people's number, they called him by his own real name: Simeon Katiti Sambo.

To read out

Injustice and inequality can make children very angry:

Angry smells like a flower burning.

Angry looks like a horrible face.

Angry sounds like a lion fierce.

Angry feels like danger!

(Bhavesh Bhudia, age 8)

Closing thoughts

O God, give food to the people who are hungry.
And make the people who *have* food hungry for the world to be fair and sharing.

(free translation of a prayer in Spanish from Uruguay)

No Difference

Small as a peanut,
Big as a giant,
We're all the same size
When we turn off the light.

Rich as a sultan,
Poor as a mite,
We're all worth the same
When we turn off the light.

Red, black or orange,
Yellow or white,
We all look the same
When we turn off the light.

So maybe the way
To make everything right
Is for God to reach out
And turn off the light!

(Shel Silverstein, *Where the Sidewalk Ends*, Harper and Row, 1974, p. 81)

This is written very much from a child's point of view and should ideally be read by children. The piece is constructed in a series of pairs of thoughts and it seems obvious to involve pairs of children as readers. Yet it needs to be a fairly contemplative time and too many pairs of child readers would be very distracting for the rest of the children. Two accomplished readers – a girl and a boy – reading alternate lines are more likely to create the desired atmosphere.

Dear God,
The world is so big and I am so small.
The problems all around are really great and I am only little.
I see people hurt by others and I cannot help them.
I see people doing wrong and I cannot stop them.
I hear of soldiers fighting wars and I cannot end them.
I hear of babies without food and I cannot feed them.
I know of people sad and lonely and I cannot reach them.
I know of people sick and dying and I cannot heal them.

Please keep telling me that there are other people who care like me and we can work together.
Please keep telling me that you care about us all and you will help us do it.

Then the world could be a bit more the way you would like it.
Then the world could be a bit better because I was in it.

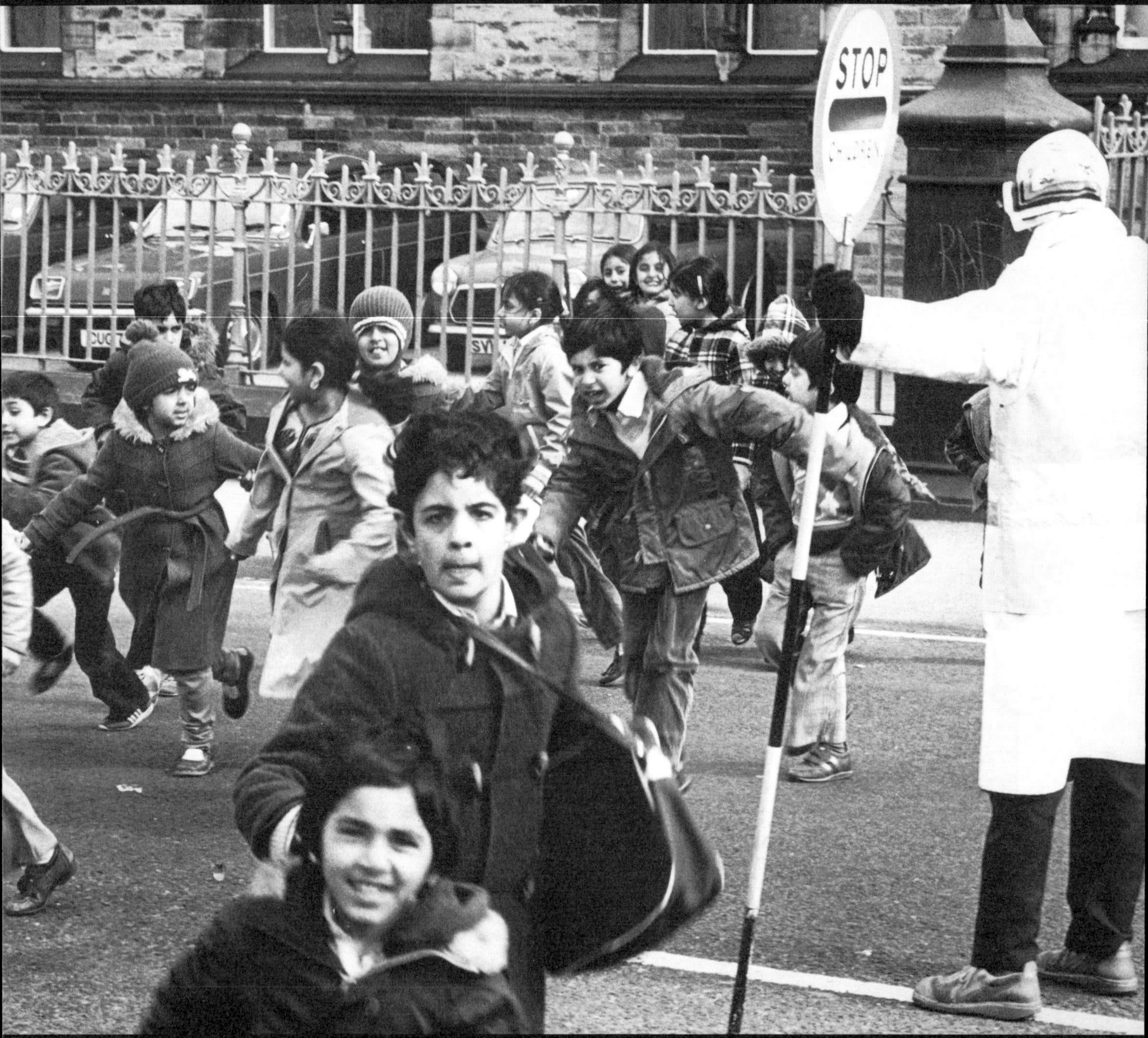
STOP
CHILDREN

11
Flying high!

Everybody wants to be free – or do they? Free at any price? Paradoxically, it is making a firm commitment and focusing our life most sharply that may give us a greater sense of freedom, than drifting without purpose or hope.

hope and freedom

An activity

One of the following thought-provoking or contemplative stimuli might introduce the theme:

Share with the children a variety of ways – and a range of reasons – in which we experience that we are not free, e.g. accidentally getting locked in toilet, kept in during play, unable to see some films at the cinema before a certain age, having to wear school uniform/not allowed to wear jewellery or a watch . . .

Stage a simple tableau of 'un-freedom' with children in any or all of the following situations: boxed in by chairs with slatted backs; holding an oven rack or grille in front of their face; hands tied together (loosely!) with skipping rope; gagged (slightly!) with silk scarf; chained to each other with newspaper links . . .

If the school has three hamsters, set up three tables (or a long table with three areas) about 40–50 cm high. Place on the table (1) a hamster in a cage with plenty of food; (2) food and a hamster which is allowed to roam freely on the table top but in a small area; and (3) a hamster without any food allowed to roam freely over a large area. Encourage the children to watch the hamsters intently and silently. Afterwards, you may ask them to register in their own mind in which situation the hamster was most free; or you may invite them to share their observations aloud; or they may be permitted to react in a completely free way to what they saw.

(Hamsters are generally affectionate and tolerant of humans and hardly ever bite but because they have such a keen sense of smell and are fiercely individualistic, you would be unwise to cross-handle, that is, handle one hamster after another! Have the three hamsters handled by different children/colleagues.)

If you have only one hamster, place it for a few minutes in each of the three situations in turn.)

To read out

Being free is not always wonderful: sometimes freedom is scary and not at all as cosy as being kept in. Wilbur was a pig kept in a pen on a farm owned by the Zuckermans. His best human friend was a girl called Fern, but he also had some animal friends who lived outside the pen and could move freely.

One day a goose noticed that a plank of wood on Wilbur's pen had come loose and she told him that if he pushed it he could escape and see what a wonderful place the world is. He took her advice, broke out and started skipping and prancing all over the farm; soon all the farmers were trying to catch Wilbur! When the animals heard what had happened, they went wild with excitement that he was free and started shouting to him lots of suggestions for getting away from the farmers. This confused and exhausted Wilbur, who was already pining for Fern to comfort him, and he started to cry.

'Come, pig!' said Mr Zuckerman, tapping the pail. 'Come, pig!'

Wilbur took a step towards the pail. 'No-no-no!' said the goose. 'I't the old pail trick, Wilbur. Don't fall for it, don't fall for it! He's trying to lure you back into captivity-ivity. He's appealing to your stomach.'

Wilbur didn't care. The food smelled appetising. He took another step towards the pail. 'Pig, pig!' said Mr Zuckerman in a kind voice, and began walking slowly towards the barnyard, looking all about him innocently, as if he didn't know that a little white pig was following along behind him.

'You'll be sorry-sorry-sorry,' called the goose. Wilbur didn't care. He kept walking towards the pail of slops.

'You'll miss your freedom,' honked the goose. 'An hour of freedom is worth a barrel of slops.' Wilbur didn't care. ●

When Mr Zuckerman reached the pigpen, he climbed over the fence and poured the slops into the trough. Then he pulled the loose board away from the fence, so that there was a wide hole for Wilbur to walk through.

'Reconsider, reconsider!' cried the goose. Wilbur paid no attention. He stepped through the fence into his yard. He walked to the trough and took a long drink of slops, sucking in the milk hungrily and chewing the popover. It was good to be home again.

While Wilbur ate, Lurvy fetched a hammer and some eight-penny nails and nailed the board in place. Then he and Mr Zuckerman leaned lazily on the fence and Mr Zuckerman scratched Wilbur's back with a stick. 'He's quite a pig,' said Lurvy.

'Yes, he'll make a good pig,' said Mr Zuckerman. Wilbur heard the words of praise. He felt the warm milk inside his stomach. He felt the pleasant rubbing of the stick along his itchy back. He felt peaceful and happy and sleepy. This had been a tiring afternoon. It was still only about four o'clock but Wilbur was ready for bed.

'I'm really too young to go out into the world alone,' he thought as he lay down.

(E. B. White, *Charlotte's Web*, Puffin Books, 1952/88, 0 14 030185 2, pp. 26–28.)

Closing thought

We cannot *do* or *have* exactly what we want all the time. But we can *think* and *feel* exactly what we want at any time. We can even choose *not* to be free if we want to.

Mix and match

The video

Clip number 11 on the accompanying video cassette concerns the breaking down of the Berlin Wall. We do not know whether the wall will *stay* down for ever – and no other walls of its kind be built either – and whether its fall will reunite everyone who was divided and usher in universal freedom. But the destruction of the wall is a key experience in modern history which resonated across the globe and is likely to become an event of mythical significance.

It may seem that the history of the political situation is too complex for the children but they do need some background to appreciate the impact of the event. It can be visualised for them quite easily by setting up a table with a row of egg boxes (or something else that can be easily bashed!) to represent a wall in the middle, running from back to front. As most maps have north at the top, make West Germany on the left-hand side, from the children's point of view, and East Germany on the right. As you describe what happened, you can point to each side in turn or, better still, use dolls or people models. And don't resist the temptation to knock the wall down at the end!

This is about a surprise that made many people very happy and helped other people to hope that they will be free one day . . .

For nearly 30 years Germany was divided into two parts – East and West. The East German government wanted to keep their people on their side so they built a border down the middle of the country, and a thick wall right through the city of Berlin; but the West German government didn't want the wall. Then the two governments started getting friendlier and people began to hope that they would break the wall down in the end. But they never expected it to happen so soon and so suddenly!

This film has pictures in *black-and-white* which were taken when the wall was first built: some people were crying because they missed their families and some were trying to escape from East Germany to the West, where they thought they could have a better life. In West Germany, people on marches were trying to make Germany into one country again; and the banners said 'Freiheit', which means 'freedom' in German. The *colour* part of the film shows what happened when the day came to take down the wall.

To read out

This narrative poem by 14-year-old Natalie Howard may prepare the factual as well as the emotional ground:

Nearly 30 years of imprisonment,
Would that have been as bad?
Instead of living inside a wall
They were in their own little land.

No one was allowed to enter
Or exit, as the case may be.
Berlin, a re-opened town,
Was something we wanted to see.

Well, now that it has happened,
It's a little hard to believe.
Does this mean the world is changing,
Getting better, people free?

The actual event was special,
To watch the whole thing fall,
Celebrations and reunions
And a party on the wall.

These lines from a poem by 15-year-old Nina Sehdev point beyond the physical wall:

*'The wall has come down.
When will the barrier of people's
feelings come down?'*

To read out or act

Versions of this story have been attributed to both the Inuit and the Amerindian peoples. This story lends itself to very simple dramatisation or boldly declarative reading by seven children (the Wise One, her five daughters and a narrator):

At the beginning of time, when all was air, the Wise One called her daughters to her and said, 'I shall give you each a wish and you can join me in creation.'

The first wished for water, flowing forever and giving life.
The second wished for earth in which plants could take root and on which animals could roam.
The third wished for fire to give light, warmth and power.
The fourth wished for good people – to be loving, truthful and fair.
The fifth wished for bad people who would rule over the earth, proudly, bravely – and cruelly!

When the Wise One heard this, she wept. 'I so wanted a beautiful world,' she said, 'but if I grant the fifth wish it will bring evil into the world and then everything will be in danger of being destroyed by bad people. Yet I made you all free to choose your own one wish and I cannot take it back. But I, too, have a wish and I will use it now. I wish for the world the gift of hope . . .'

The song

Bless, O Maker, Bless

(This was sung unaccompanied by a multiracial group of students led by a Black African conductor and singers, at the United World College of the Atlantic, Wales; it was broadcast on the BBC television programme, 'Songs of Praise', in 1984.

The music has been transcribed by Walter Robson. Angela Wood transliterated the Xhosa lyric and wrote the English version.)

Moderately

Bless, O Ma-ker, bless this land of ours. Raise her high in hon-our
Koh'-see si-ke-leyl ee' - Af - ri - ka. Ma-loo-pa-ka-nees-oo

and in glo-ry. Lis-ten to our prayers when we call you.
*doo-moh lwa-yoh. Yis-way ee-mee-tan-da-zoh yeh'-too.

Give us per-fect bless-ing: We are her sons and daugh-ters.
Koh' - see si-ke-ley-la: Tee - na loo-sa-poh lwa-yoh.

Ho-ly Spi-rit, Ho-ly   Ho-ly Spi-rit, Ho-ly
Wo-za mo-ya, Wo-za   Wo-za mo-ya, Wo-za
Come, Ho-ly One,   Come, Ho-ly One,
Wo-za mo-ya,   Wo-za mo-ya,

Come, Ho-ly One, Ho-ly One, Ho-ly One. Give us
Wo-za mo-ya, Oh' yee' g - weh - ley! Koh' - see

per-fect bless-ing: We are her sons and daugh-ters. May the Lord keep safe-ly the
si-ke-ley-la: Tee - na loo-sa-poh lwa-yoh. Mo-rey-na bo-lo-ka seh'

peo-ple that we love! May our quar-rels stop and all our trou-bles end!
cha-ba sa heh' soh! Oh'-feh'-dee-seh din-twah leh ma-tswen-ye-hoh!

* In some versions, 'oofondoh' is sung.

Book box

Jeannette Caines, *Daddy*, Harper and Row, 1977, 0 06 020923 2. A child lives with her mother and only sees her father when he comes to collect her on Saturdays.

Anthony Browne, *Bear Hunt*, Hippo Books, 1982, 0 590 70090 1. With his magic pencil, Bear can create anything he wants; he is able to save animals from being hunted and effect his own escape on the wings of a bird!

Babette Cole, *Princess Smartypants*, Picture Lions, 1986, 0 00 662798 6. Wishing to be free of gender stereotyping and of the royal expectations placed upon her, the princess sets the inevitable suitors tasks which she hopes they will find impossible to achieve, such as taking her mother shopping . . .

Robert D. San Souci, *The Enchanted Tapestry*, Dial Books, 1987, 0 8037 0862 9. A delicately illustrated Chinese folktale concerning a widow who weaves hopes and dreams into a tapestry . . .

Virginia Hamilton, 'The People Could Fly', in *The People Could Fly: American Black Folktales*, Walker Books, 1988, 0 7445 0524 0, pp. 166–73. A moving story about slaves.

Meshack Asare, *The Canoe's Story*, Miracle Bookhouse, 1982, 0 9964 961 03. A powerful story from Ghana about a personified tree who is cut down and wonders why.

An activity

Ask everyone to close their eyes and read this to them four times altogether: the first reading is straight through; before the second reading, ask everyone to pick out in their mind, as you read the lines, the words they like; the third time, ask everyone to say out loud the words they like as you read them; the fourth time, ask everyone to say the lines along with you – they will almost certainly know them by now!

Some people had to hide in a cold, dark cellar for safety. We do not know their names but this is what they wrote:

I believe in the sun even when it is not shining.
I believe in love even when feeling it not.
I believe in God even when he is silent.

Closing thoughts

The Holocaust was a time of great despair, yet also a time of great hope. It may be inappropriate to introduce it to some children, yet many can grasp the essence of that experience, which has become a landmark of the twentieth century, and derive meaning and value from it.

About 50 years ago, many countries in Europe were taken over by selfish, bossy people called Nazis who were so cruel that they thought there were certain kinds of people who did not deserve to be alive. They especially did not like Jews. Whenever the Nazis found the people they did not like, they took them away, first to work hard with very little food, and then to be killed.

It must have been very difficult to think about good things and happy times then, but some people did and we are lucky that what they said or wrote was kept safely for us to hear now.

Some men had to march a long way from one work place to the next and couldn't even remember when they had last had something

to eat or drink. One of them was with his teenage son and wanted him to believe that they *could* go on living and that life would be better. He said to him:

'You can live three weeks without food. You can live three days without water. But you cannot live three minutes without hope.'

Anne Frank was a teenage girl who had to hide with her family and friends in an attic. For a while, some kind brave people brought them food but in the end they were discovered and they were taken away. All of them except Anne's father died. Anne had kept a diary and left it behind in the attic, and her father found it when he was freed, several years later. Anne used to love looking up through the tiny roof window at the sky and seeing birds fly across it. Perhaps she wrote this then:

'I believe that people are really good at heart . . . If I look into the heavens I think that it will all come out right, and that peace and calm will return again . . .'

The writer of the poem 'Reformation Truth' is unknown. As in all Rastafarian writing, God has strong, majestic names and this verse says that it is God who gives freedom and that makes people feel safe!

'Thou mighty King of Kings, Thou Tree of Life,
Thou Father of the free,
Thou Elohim Jehovah Jah,
We stand secure in thee.'

(in Leonard E. Barrett, *The Rastafarians*, Heinemann, 1977, 0 435 89458 7, p. 234)

'Freedom is not being under pressure from anyone or anything. Hope is not to give up but to stay on until you're through all the hardness. It is always easy to have faith in yourself and life will not let you down until it is time to die and you have won the battle. In the end, you will be free to roam any place around. So keep up the fight and don't let it go, OK!'

(Jamie Munro, age 9)

These words of hope, which refer to the saving death of Jesus, are attributed to the Black South African leader, Archbishop Desmond Tutu:

'Goodness is stronger than evil;
Love is stronger than hate;
Light is stronger than darkness;
Life is stronger than death;
Victory is ours through Him who loved us.'

These lines, yearning for hope and all that is life-affirming, paraphrase a well-known verse from Hindu scriptures:

Lead me from death to life.
Lead me from falsehood to truth.
Lead me from despair to hope.
Lead me from fear to trust.
Lead me from hate to love.
Lead me from war to peace.

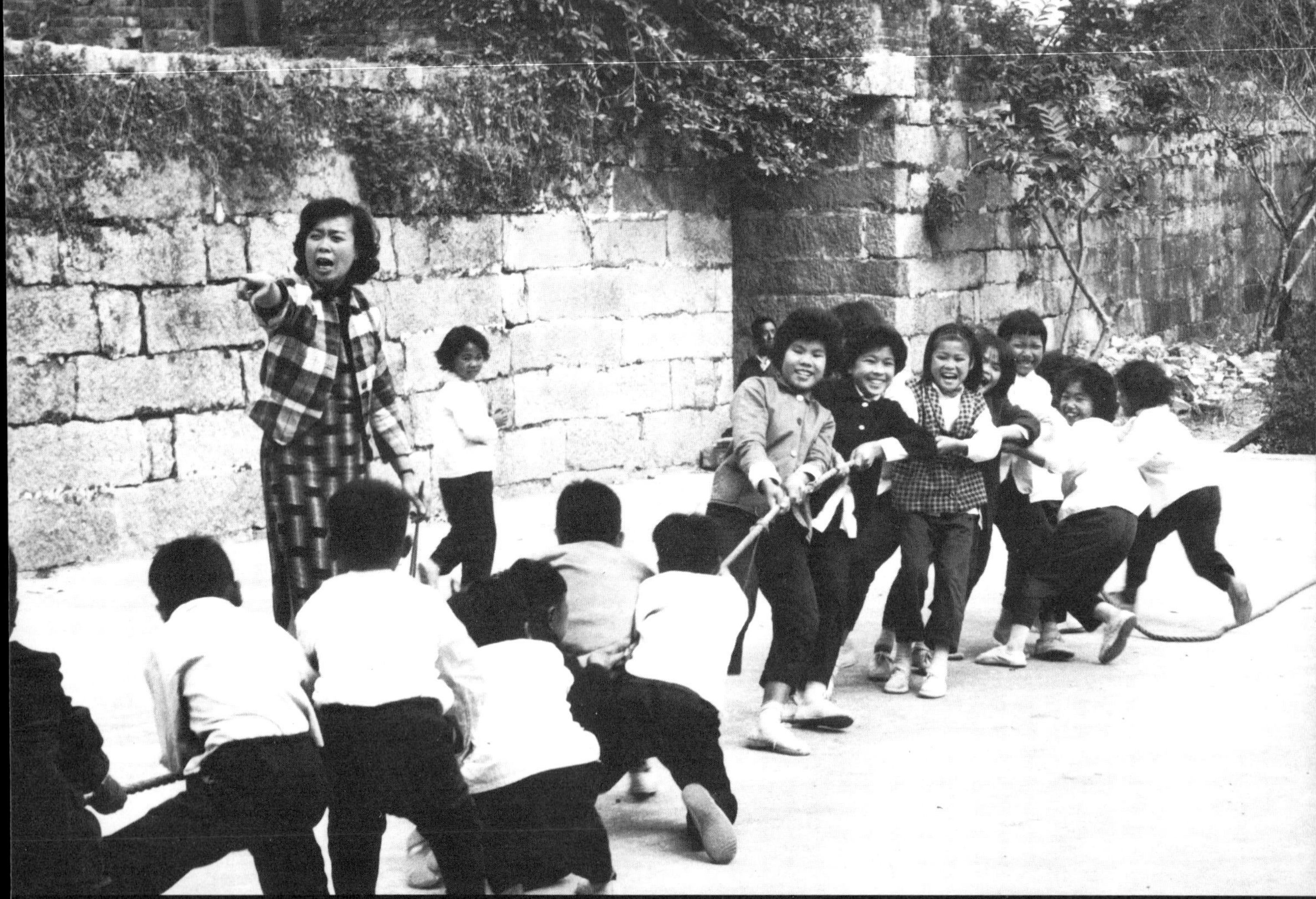

12

All in the game

Competition and cooperation raise not only the question 'Is winning everything?' but also 'What is winning, anyway? Can we lose by winning and can we win by losing?'

winning and losing

Ideally, this opening assembly should be linked to a recent or forthcoming sports match, or other competitive situation. The point might be made by the presenter appearing in games kit or just trainers, blowing a whistle to start, organising the rows of children in a commanding voice, perhaps even referring to them as 'teams' or 'sides'!

This could open a discussion about 'playing the game': if the linked event involves two teams against each other, the question could be asked: is it possible to win without someone else losing? If not, does it matter? If the occasion is, say, a presentation of cycling proficiency certificates or swimming stripes, the key question might be: did anyone beat anyone else, or just their own previous record?

To read out

This anecdote recounted and reflected upon by a girl at Primary school draws together many of these sporting questions:

The video

Clip number 12 on the accompanying video cassette is a montage from the world of sport and makes an accessible starting-point for a consideration of the theme. The sequences contain examples of success, failure, possible foul play and the ultimate in cooperation. Together they provide an opportunity to ask, 'Is winning everything in life? And what does winning mean anyway?' (It may help to show this as a whole and also in its component parts: see notes on clip number 1 on page 18.)

Sometimes we win at what we do, sometimes we lose, sometimes we have to beat *ourselves* and sometimes we can join with other people so that *everybody* wins.

You will see people playing different kinds of sport: who is winning? who is losing? is it fair?

'One day Tarik told me he would like a game of football against the girls. I said I didn't like having girls against boys so he said, "OK. You have three boys on your team and I'll have three girls on my team." We found it very hard because we don't play a lot but at the end of the game, the score was 10–2 to us!'

'I could see that Tarik was upset that his team didn't win maybe because his team often wins. It made me not so happy that we had won. I knew he had tried. I think we won because they didn't have a good goalie. All my friends were happy we'd won but I was sorry for the other team. I don't know why: it's only a game!'

(Alice Bell, age 9)

Closing thought

Winning is not always making the others lose.
Winning is not always getting a prize.
Winning is not always gaining the highest score.

Winning is also doing your best.
Winning is also playing with others.
Winning is also being fair.

Mix and match

An activity

The sense of collective success and mutual pleasure of cooperative games and tasks provide a significant experience for children in exploring issues of gain and loss. A simple example which can be tried in any classroom is 'musical non-chairs': when the music stops and a chair/cushion is removed, no child becomes 'out'. Rather the children share the cushions, sit on any part of the armchair or indeed in each other's laps. The logical conclusion is that the entire class ends up in a pile on top of one space – but in reality the situation dissolves in hysterics long before that!

Book box

Penny Dale, *Bet You Can't!*, Walker Books, 1989, 0 7445 1225 5. A brother and a sister vie with each other to carry the toybox back when they tidy up at bedtime.

Naina Gandhi, *Sari Games*, Andre Deutsch, 1990, 0 233 98543 3. A special book for the early years which demonstrates the versatility of an old blue sari for make-believe on a rainy day.

Babette Cole, *Prince Cinders*, Picture Lions, 1987, 0 00 662964 4. Role reversal of the traditional fairy tale helps the Prince win through a tricky situation.

Kiri Te Kanawa, 'Kakariki and Kaka' in *Land of the Long White Cloud* (Maori Myths, Tales and Legends), Pavilion Books, 1989, 1 85145 176 5, p. 115. Cheating to get red and green feathers won the day!

Edna O'Brien, 'The Leprechaun', in *Tales for the Telling* (Irish Folk and Fairy Stories), Puffin Books, 1988, 0 14 032293 0, pp. 17–20. The Leprechaun has the power to bestow wealth *and* to double-cross.

To read out

A Fish of the World

An important element in success is boasting – or perhaps rather the need to resist boasting!

Depending on the sex education policy of the school and the ages of the pupils, they will need to have spawning explained to them or be able to explain it! A globe showing the major seas and oceans would usefully demonstrate that the herring circumnavigated the world and therefore can claim in some sense to 'have been everywhere'!

Herrings are fish who usually live in the North Sea but one particular herring once grew tired of the place and, deciding to explore the seas of the world, he set off on an adventure. And an adventure he had – a really exciting though often dangerous time! Eventually he returned home to the North Sea.

'All his friends and relations gathered round and made a great fuss of him. They had a big feast and offered him the very best food they could find. But the herring just yawned and said, "I've swum round the entire world. I have seen everything there is to see, and I have eaten more exotic and wonderful dishes than you could possibly imagine." And he refused to eat anything.

Then his friends and relations begged him to come home and live with them, but he refused. "I've been everywhere there is, and that old rock is too dull and small for me." And he went off and lived on his own.

And when the breeding season came, he refused to join in the spawning, saying: "I've swum around the entire world, and now I know how many fish there are in the world, I can't be interested in herrings anymore." ●

'Eventually, one of the oldest of the herrings swam up to him, and said: "Listen. If you don't spawn with us, some herrings' eggs will go unfertilised and will not turn into healthy young herrings. If you don't live with your family, you'll make them sad. And if you don't eat, you'll die."

112

'But the herring said: "I don't mind. I've been everywhere there is to go, I've seen everything there is to see, and now I know everything there is to know."

The old fish shook his head. "No one has ever seen everything there is to see," he said, "nor known everything there is to know."

"Look," said the herring, "I've swum through the North Sea, the Atlantic Ocean, the Indian Ocean, the Java Sea, the Coral Sea, the great Pacific Ocean, the Siberian Sea and the frozen Arctic. Tell me, what else is there for me to see or know?"

"I don't know," said the old herring, "but there may be something." ▲

Well, just then a fishing-boat came by, and all the herrings were caught in a net and taken to market that very day. And a man bought the herring, and ate it for his supper.

And he never knew that it had swum right round the world, and had seen everything there was to see, and knew everything there was to know.'

(Terry Jones, 'A Fish of the World', in *Fairy Tales*, Puffin Books, 1981, 0 14 03164 26, pp. 69–71)

To read out

Winning and losing are inevitably bound up with humility, greed and the just reward – as exemplified in this folk-tale which is now identifiably Creole but was possibly transmitted by French émigrés who settled in Louisiana.

All day long the mother and her elder daughter would sit on the front porch of their wooden house, dreaming they were fine ladies, dancing all night at the most fashionable balls in the land! Yet they were poor and would have been even poorer if the younger daughter had not worked her tiny fingers to the bone, feeding the chickens, plucking the little cotton they were able to grow and scratching in the ground for potatoes.

One day she was at the well in the wood, filling her bucket for her sister who had demanded a cool drink, when an old lady asked for a sip of water. The girl offered her the whole pail and the woman drank deep and long. 'You have a beautiful soul, my child,' she said, 'and God's blessings will fall upon you.' And with that she disappeared. ●

'Aah! Are you trying to burn me to death?' shrieked her sister when she passed her the bucket of water. 'I told you to get me a *cool* drink but this is absolutely boiling!' And indeed it was! Her mother was so angry that she took off her shoe and began thwacking her across the face so hard that the little girl ran off into the woods, sobbing.

Soon she met the old woman again who said she could come and stay with her for the night as long as she promised not to laugh at any of the strange things where the woman lived: a two-headed cow that brayed like a donkey; rabbits that danced, sang and played the guitar; and multicoloured chickens that whistled and had anything from one to a hundred legs. But the young girl did not make fun of them even when the elderly woman actually took off her head to comb her hair! It was truly a magical place and a rich stew was miraculously cooked from just a bone and a huge bowl of rice from a single grain. ▲

The next morning, the old woman described to the girl two kinds of eggs that she would find in the chicken house – some of precious stones that called out, 'Don't take me!' and some ordinary hens' eggs that called out, 'Take me!' She could take the plain ones and should throw them over her shoulder one by one, as she made her way home.

The jewels were very tempting, but she had promised . . . so she carefully gathered up the hens' eggs and began the journey back. To her amazement and delight, each one she tossed away turned into a silk dress, a pair of satin shoes, a velvet cloak, a gold necklace . . . ■

When her mother saw her returning with treasure, greed overcame her. So she told her elder daughter to get whatever she could – however she could – from the old lady. When she arrived, she saw the cow, the chickens and the rabbits and collapsed with laughter; she too boiled a bone in a pot but all she got was boiled bone! She too cooked a grain of rice but all she got was a grain of rice! When the elderly woman took off her head to comb her hair, the horrid girl snatched it and stuck it on a railing. Then she rushed into the chicken house and, ignoring what the eggs said, grabbed as many jewelled ones as she could, and raced back to show her mother, chuckling as she ran, 'Aha! Now we'll live in luxury for the rest of our lives . . .'

Along the way, she tossed each of the eggs in turn over her shoulder – but imagine her horror when they were transformed not into fine robes and precious jewels but poisonous snakes and vicious beasts!

(One of the variations on this story is beautifully told and realistically illustrated in Robert D. San Souci, *The Talking Eggs*, Bodley Head, 1989, 0 370 31382 8.)

The song

Taking Sides

This song is based on the story of the same title by Angela Wood, *Faith Stories for Today*, BBC/Longman, 1990, 0 582 05946 1, pp. 28–33. In this Sikh story set amid religious conflict, the real victory is seen to lie not in the death of religious opponents but in the sense of a common humanity.

(A drone on a synthesiser – a chord of C – helps enormously, as does simple percussion.)

NARRATOR:
Many died that day in battle and at dusk one man, Khaneeya, was to be seen walking across the battlefield alone.

VOICES:
That very night when the fighting was done
Khaneeya found some men alive,
Knowing deep down that nobody had won
Khaneeya helped them to survive.
And the hope
That he brought
To the wounded
Gave a night of peace to all the men who fought
For their faith.

NARRATOR:
But Khaneeya's comrades saw that he was not only giving water to their own wounded, but also to the soldiers of the enemy. They were furious and went to see Guru Gobind Singh Ji, to complain.

VOICES:
All through the day we all risked our lives,
Until we had no more to give,
Fought for our faith and our children and wives;
He helps the other side to live.
What's the use?
Who is right?
Is he crazy?
Can't you see he undermines the daily fight
For our faith?

NARRATOR:
Guru Gobind Singh Ji was a cautious man. He listened to the men very carefully and then asked Khaneeya to come and see him. He asked Khaneeya why he was helping the enemy's soldiers and Khaneeya told him.

VOICES:
I see a field that is covered in men,
But pain and fear is all I see.
They may be men who don't hold with our faith
But they're just men like you and me.
I believe
Just like you,
In my own way
Each must find their special way of staying true
To their faith.

NARRATOR:
Guru Gobind Singh Ji's eyes filled with tears and he hugged Khaneeya tightly. He saw the depth of Khaneeya's understanding of their faith and gave him bandages so that Khaneeya might carry on his work for the wounded of both sides.

VOICES:
There are some times when we all have to choose
How we can show what we believe.
It's not about if you win or you lose
It's more what you give and receive.
So we learn,
Me and you,
Like Khaneeya
Each must find a special way of staying true
To their faith.

Notes on 'Taking Sides'

The drone is very important to this song. This can easily be done using a synthesiser or cello playing a low chord of C. In place of a sitar, a flute or even kazoo or comb and tissue paper can be used to double the melody line to give it an Indian flavour. Percussion (bongos or small tom-toms and Indian bells) also help to carry the song along.

The use of a Narrator in the song could be developed into the story of the song being acted out by some of the class while the others are singing and playing it.

The words and music were especially written for *Assembly Kit* by Stephen Clark and the music was transcribed by Kate Buchanan.

1 All through the day they fought for their breath Until the ground was churned to mud.
  All through the day they fought to the death Until the ground was turned to blood. And the men On each side Showed no mercy, When the sun had set they counted those who died, For their faith.

Closing thoughts

Exams

I hate exams;
The questions don't always seem fair
Sometimes they're too hard anyway.
I suppose we've got to have them,
But I wish we didn't:
Teachers always say it will be all right
If we've worked!
I haven't always worked hard, but who does,
Apart from you, Lord?
I don't want special favours,
But help me and my form
To do as well as we can
And certainly as well as we deserve.

(Louise Carpenter (ed.), *The Puffin Book of Prayers*, 1990, 0 14 034348 2, p. 46)

Helen Keller was deaf and blind from birth but she decided she wanted to be one of life's successes, not one of life's failures. She once wrote:

'I believe that God is in me as the sun is in the colour and the scent of a flower. God is the light in my darkness and the voice in my silence.'

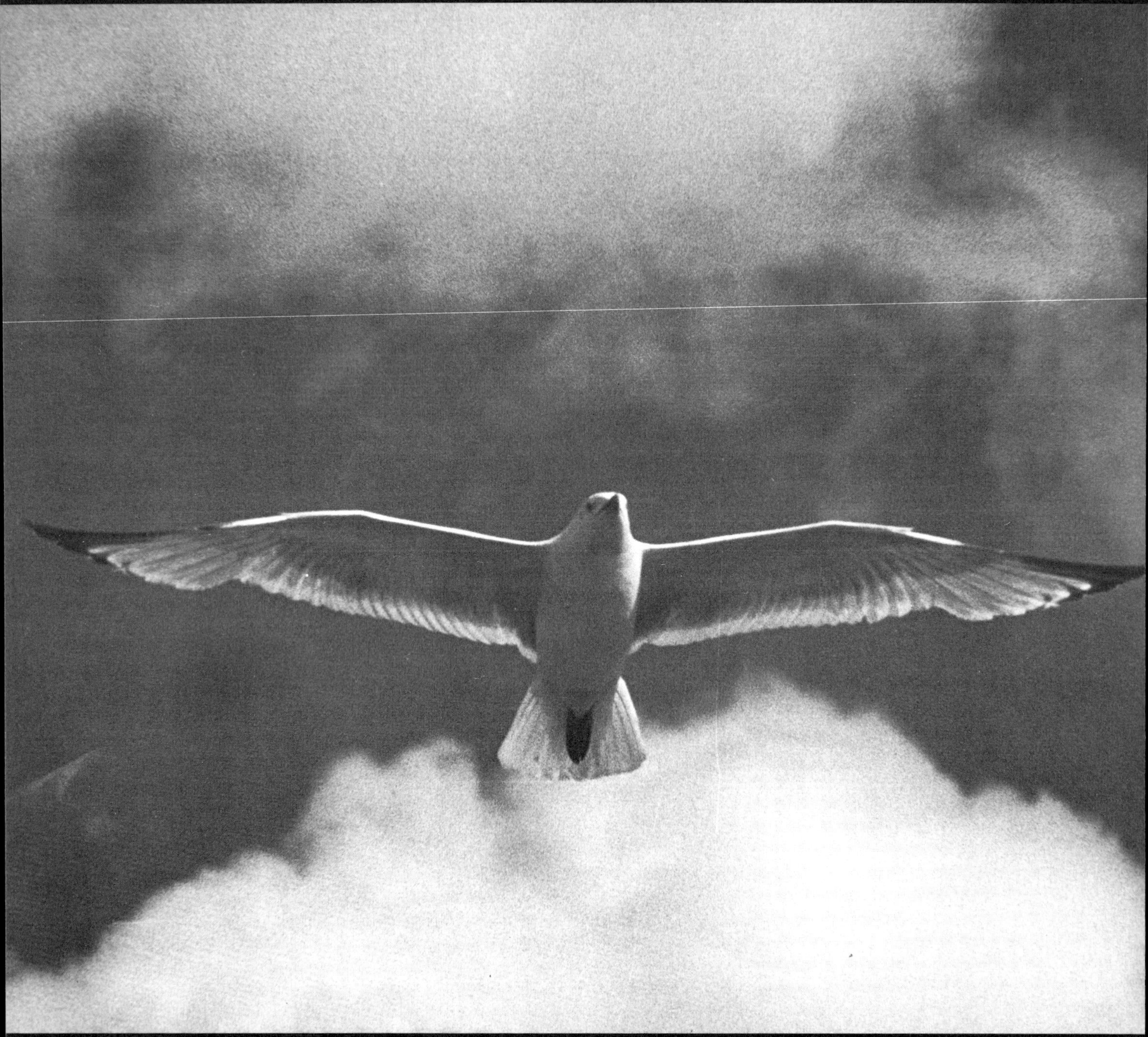

13
You can do it

Religion sometimes represses certain human capacities as well as generating and developing them. So does education! The need to find out what we really are – and could be! – brings religion and education together.

struggle, determination and survival

To read out

Although *Jonathan Livingston Seagull* is seemingly intended for older children and adults, quite young children are intrigued by Jon's vision and personal power, and identify with his need to come to terms with his smallness in the universe. Photographs of seagulls help enormously.

Jonathan Livingston Seagull always wondered about being a bird. He saw older gulls quite content to scrabble for fish but he thought there was something more important and exciting to do with his life. He wanted to fly high, to explore the world and to find out about *himself*! He believed that if you only have little thoughts, you will only ever do little things. You have to push your thoughts to make you do big things!

Some of the seagulls Jon met seemed to come from another world that was so special he felt it must be heaven. Other gulls thought *he* was especially wise or good, like God, the Great Gull. He said you have to see the good in everyone, the real gull, and help them see it in themselves – that's what love is!

"Chiang, this world isn't heaven, is it?"

The Elder smiled in the moonlight. "You are learning again, Jonathan Seagull," he said.

"Well, what happens from here? Where are we going? Is there no such place as heaven?"

"No, Jonathan, there is no such place. Heaven is not a place, and it is not a time. Heaven is being perfect." He was silent for a moment. "You're a very fast flier, aren't you? . . . You will begin to touch heaven, Jonathan, in the moment that you touch perfect speed. And that isn't flying a thousand miles an hour, or a million, or flying at the speed of light. Because any number is a limit, and perfection doesn't have limits. Perfect speed, my son, is being there."

Without warning, Chiang vanished and appeared at the water's edge fifty feet away, all in the flicker of an instant. Then he vanished again and stood, in the same millisecond, at Jonathan's shoulder. "It's kind of fun," he said.

(Richard Bach, *Jonathan Livingston Seagull*, Pan, 1972, 0 330 23647 4, p. 55)

Closing thought

We are like Jonathan Livingston Seagull and his friends. We can do and think and feel so much more. We can help each other to see the special person inside each of us, the real me and you – and make it grow! We can give each other beautiful thoughts and feelings that can live for ever.

This quotation works best if it is recited, then discussed, then reflected on quietly, then recited again: it would be helpful to have the quotation displayed.

'The gull who sees farthest is the one that flies the highest.'

Mix and match

The video

The squirrel sequence – clip number 13 on the accompanying video cassette – captivates children of all ages who marvel at the creature's persistence, cheer him on as he tackles the assault course and squeal with delight when he gets what he rightly earned! Be prepared for demands to show it again and again! (It may help to give the children a feel for 20 seconds and 45 feet, which is over 10 metres.)

When something is really hard to do, we often give up trying but the squirrel in this story was absolutely determined not to be beaten! It took two weeks to work out how to get to the food but then it took only twenty seconds to repeat it! Look at all the obstacles that were in the way and count how many difficult things the squirrel has to do.

To read out or act

The well-loved traditional Jain story of the four daughters-in-law and five grains of rice is a parable of struggle against the elements, of determination to do what is right and required, and of ethical survival. It will make a bold contribution to this theme, especially if it is mimed to the narration or enacted, as it can be simply scripted. As props, you will need 20 grains of rice (in theory – more in practice!), a cooking pot (preferably Indian), a decorated box such as for jewels, improvised carts (such as push-chairs or trolleys) and sacks or bags stuffed with newspapers or some such. There are nine characters though only five have real roles: a father and his four daughters-in-law (plus the four sons!). Asian clothing should be worn if available or possible to improvise. If feasible, have two acting areas – the father's house and the homes of the daughters-in-law.

A man was very worried about what would happen to his wealth after he died: who would be the best person to entrust it to? So he set a test: he carefully counted out into the hand of each daughter-in-law five grains of uncooked rice, speaking exactly the same words to each one, 'Look after these for me and give them back when I ask for them.'

The whole idea was crazy to the first daughter-in-law and, as she and her husband had plenty of rice, the grains weren't worth very much to her, so she threw them away. She thought that if her father-in-law ever did ask for the grains back, she could always go and get some from their barn. ●

The second wife couldn't be bothered with the five grains at all and threw them into a pot she was cooking at the time. They also had a huge store of rice and she could get some out any time she needed to.

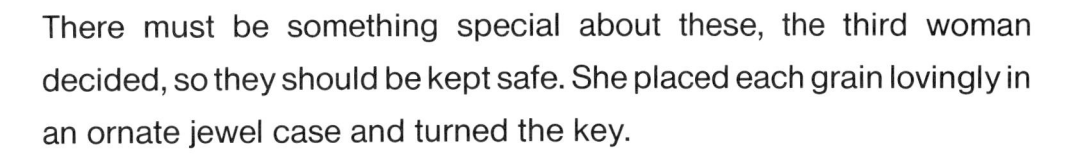

There must be something special about these, the third woman decided, so they should be kept safe. She placed each grain lovingly in an ornate jewel case and turned the key.

The last son's wife planted the rice in a plot which she tilled near their house: the rains made them sprout and the sun made them strong and soon there was a good harvest. She wisely held back some seed grain to plant again, washed it, dried it and saved it carefully till the next season. When she planted it, there was an even bigger crop, then she saved some seed grain again . . . and so she went on tilling, planting, reaping, washing, drying . . . ▲

. . . until one day, five years later, all four women were called back to their father-in-law who asked them for the five grains he had given them in the first place. The first two had to take rice from their store and couldn't really pretend that it was the grain they'd first been given! The third daughter-in-law brought her heavy, expensive jewel case and opened it to show that the five grains were still there, more or less.

Then the last wife arrived, empty-handed. 'Why haven't you brought back your grains?' her father-in-law asked.

'I could've,' she answered, 'but I would need several carts to bring all the sacks!' and she explained what happened.

Which woman worked hardest? which one never gave up? and which one do you think the father-in-law decided to trust with his money when he died?

To read out

It is unwise to say that 1:25 is the same as about one in every class, as some children are likely to 'look for' the one dyslexic in their own class; but a line of twenty-five random people helps visualise the proportion. The first part of the extract works well as a dialogue between a woman and a boy.

We all need to be able to read and write properly but some people have trouble getting it all together in their head. Maybe they suffer from dyslexia: one out of twenty-five people do. This was written by a ten-year-old boy who discovered he was dyslexic and did something about it!

Through the Eyes of a Dyslexic

'So, I've got a disease, ha?'

'No,' said my mum, 'you haven't got a disease . . .'

'So what does it mean, am I really thick or something?'

'No, just the opposite, the tests say you're really smart.'

By this time I was ready to scream.

'So why can't I do things as fast as other kids?'

'Because you're a dyslexic.'

'Is there a medicine to make it better?'

'No, we can't just make it go away, but we're going to send you to some classes which will teach you some tricks to overcome dyslexia.'

'I don't want to go to any dumb classes! And I don't want to be dyslexic!' ●

Well, I did go to those classes. I think the first term was a disaster . . . It was like a nightmare, and I still didn't want to know about being dyslexic. In fact I didn't want anyone to know I was dyslexic, especially my friends. Some of them were really nice about it, but some laughed at me. It really made me want to punch them in the face, but I didn't. I cried myself to sleep a lot. My mum and dad helped with things like homework and stuff . . .

In September I changed classes and met Mrs Bently, but I could never remember her name, so she wrote it on my hand. I thought it was pretty cool, because I am not allowed to write on my hands! I don't know when it happened, but things must have just clicked. By March I was up to my own level in writing and reading. In fact my school teacher said that I was doing so well he was surprised I was still going to the classes.

My mum said I should keep going because my brain's capable of doing even more than my age says I am. I know that some really smart people are dyslexic, and I don't think I'm any Einstein or anything and some days I get really fed up because things don't make sense. But as I see it, being dyslexic isn't going to stop me doing anything or being anyone I want to be when I grow up.

(Justin Hydes, in The Dyslexia Institute (ed.), *As I see It*, Walker Books, 1990, 0 7445 1601 3, p. 20)

The song

You and Me

The composer of this Hebrew song is unknown. The music has been transcribed by Walter Robson and the Hebrew transliterated by Angela Wood who also wrote the English version.

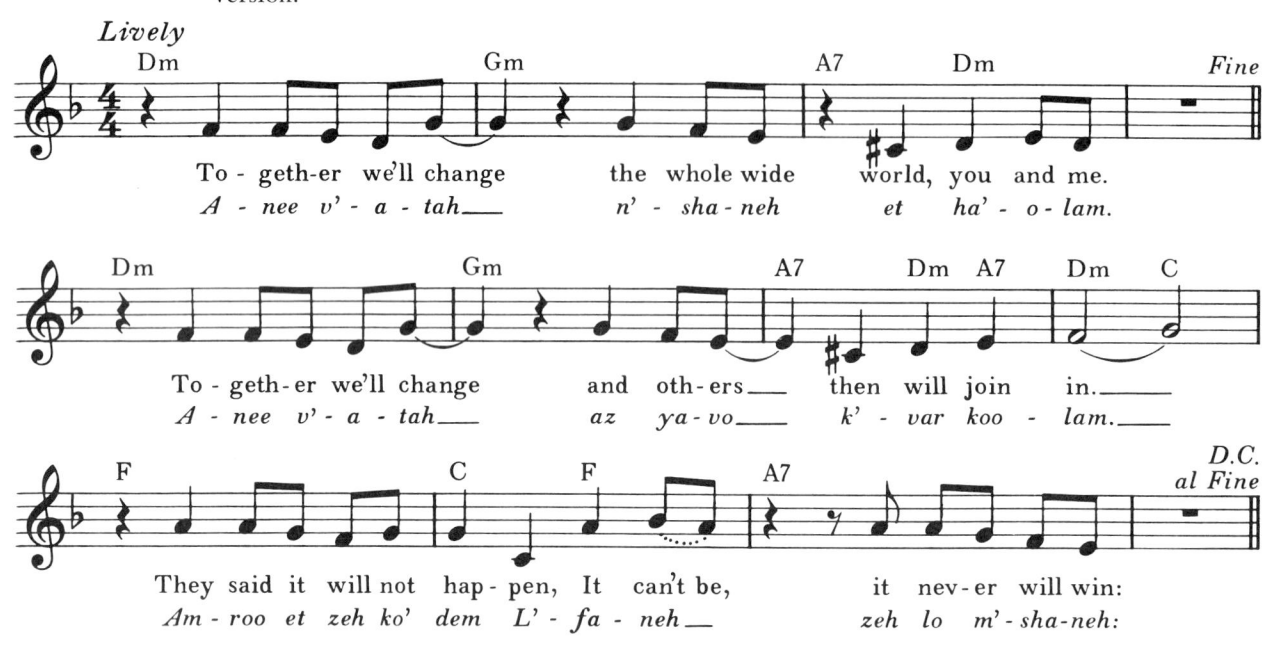

Lively

To-geth-er we'll change the whole wide world, you and me.
A - nee v' - a - tah n' - sha - neh et ha' - o - lam.

To-geth-er we'll change and oth-ers then will join in.
A - nee v' - a - tah az ya - vo k' - var koo - lam.

They said it will not hap-pen, It can't be, it nev-er will win:
Am - roo et zeh ko' dem L' - fa - neh zeh lo m' - sha - neh:

Book box

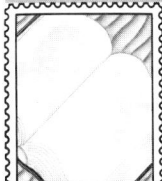

Tomie de Paola, *Oliver Button is a Sissy*, Magnet, 0 416 24540 4. Oliver doesn't like playing football but he is determined to do well at what *he* has chosen.

Tomie de Paola, *Now One Foot, Now the Other*, Methuen, 1982, 0 416 22210 2. Bob taught his grandson, Bobby, to walk ('Now one foot, now the other'), told him stories and they were the best of friends.

Ken Brown, *Why Can't I Fly?*, Doubleday, 1990, 0 385 41208 8. An ostrich who is determined to fly goes to extraordinary lengths.

Irene Hedlund, *Mighty Mountain and the Three Strong Women*, A. and C. Black, 1984, 0 590 70498 2. Told and illustrated in traditional Japanese style, this witty, original tale concerns a girl, her mother, grandmother and a seasoned wrestler.

Wendy Boase, *Billy Goats Gruff*, Walker, 1983, 0 7445 00177 6. A well-known folk story available in many other versions.

Veronique Tadjo, *Lord of the Dance*, A. and C. Black, 1988, 0 7136 3051 5. Loosely related to the hymn, this is a story about Senufo culture in the Ivory Coast.

Malcolm Carrick, *I Can Squash Elephants*, Viking, 1978, 0 670 38983 8. A Masai tale, humorously illustrated to satirise modern life.

Robert Mathias, 'The Tortoise and the Hare', in *Aesop's Fables*, Hamlyn, 1983, 0 600 38914 6. Available in many other versions, this cautionary tale is about the value of plodding!

Closing thought

Jack and Jill Be Nimble

Jack be nimble, Jack be quick,
Jack jump over the candlestick!

Jill be nimble, jump it too,
If Jack can do it, so can you!

(Douglas W. Larche, *Father Gander Nursery Rhymes*, Advocacy Press, 1985, 0 911655 12 3, p. 8)

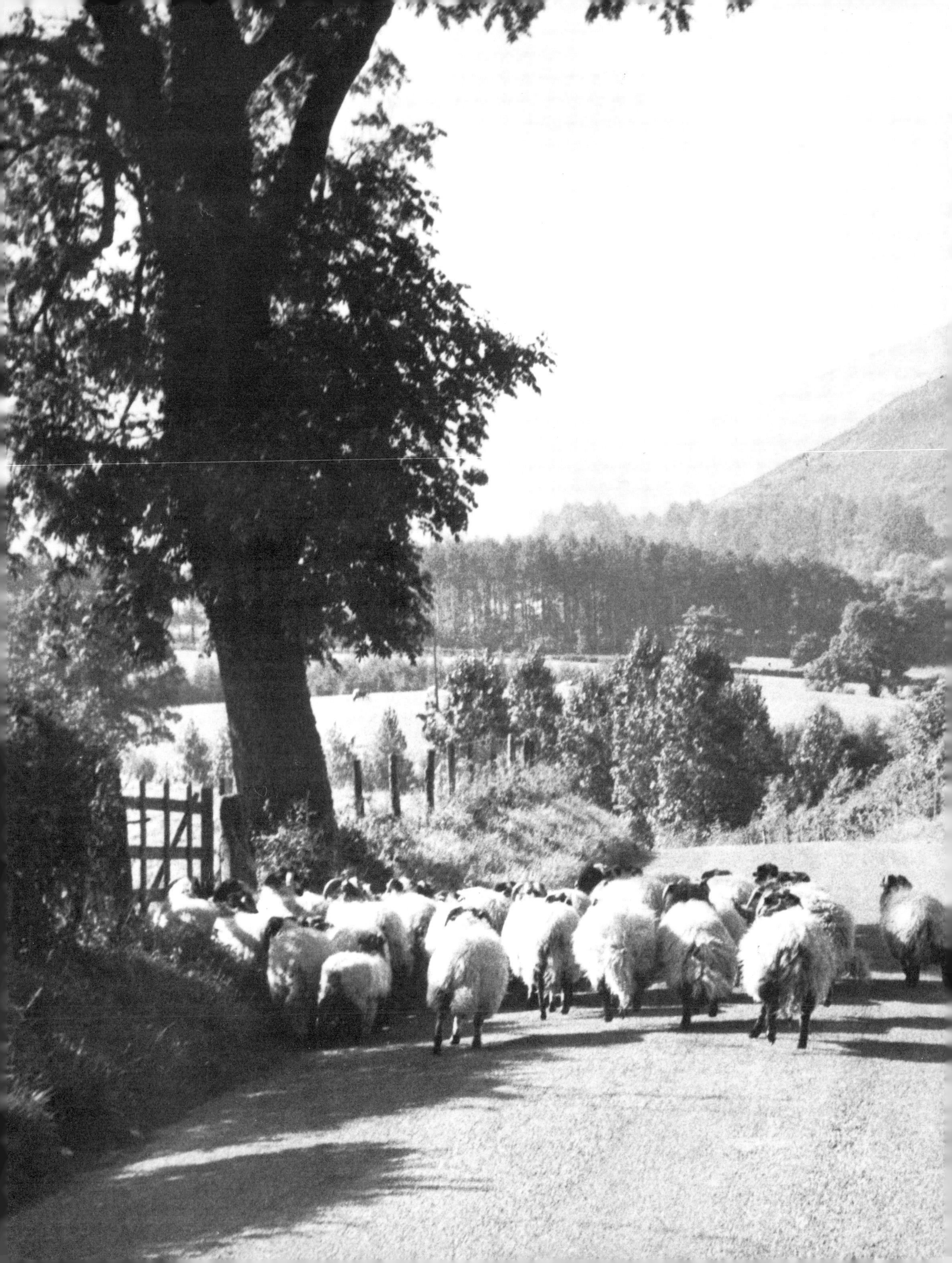

14

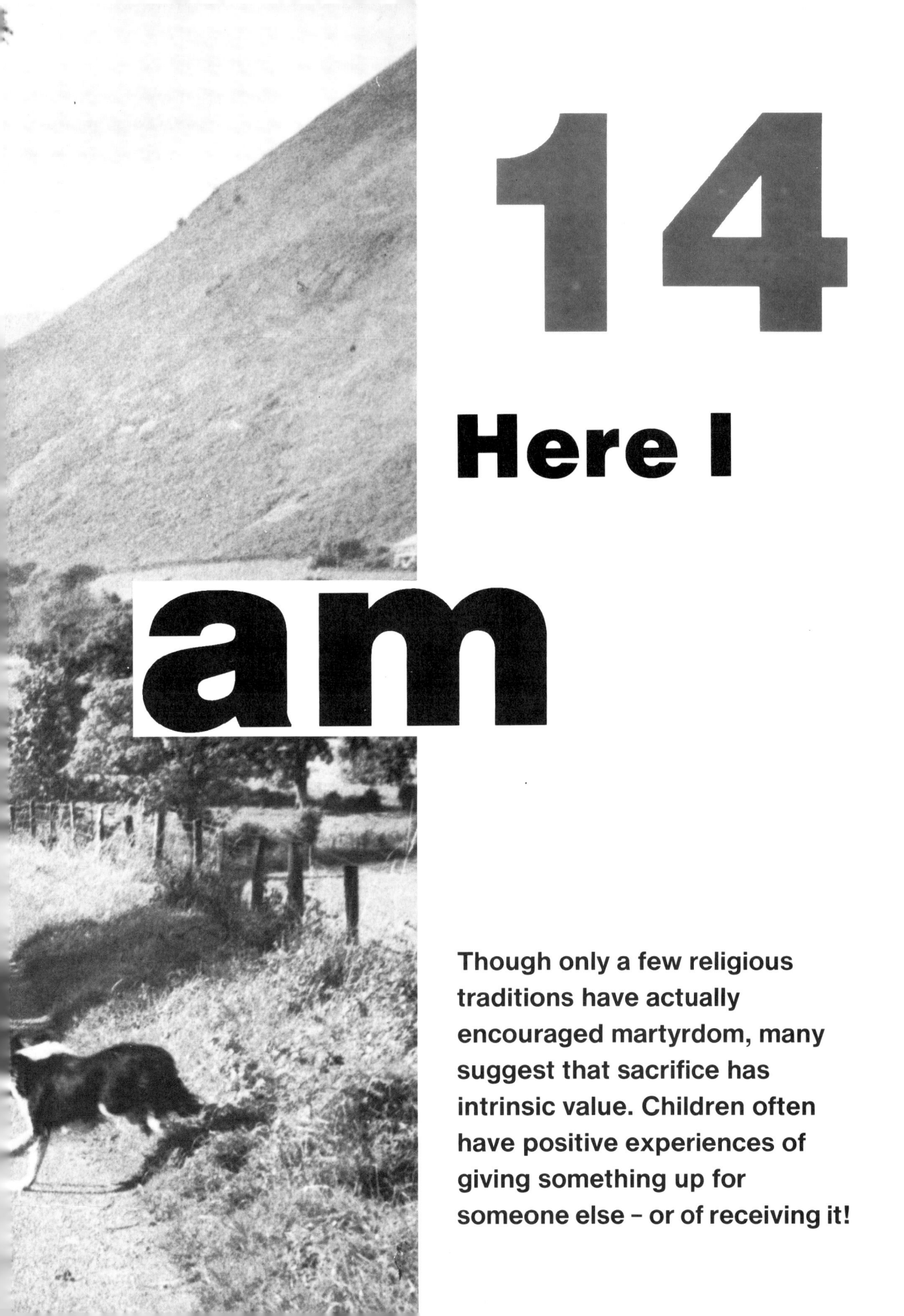

Here I am

Though only a few religious traditions have actually encouraged martyrdom, many suggest that sacrifice has intrinsic value. Children often have positive experiences of giving something up for someone else – or of receiving it!

sacrifice and courage

An activity

Before the children come in, create a structure that suggests the banks of a river with a narrow bridge between them. The 'bridge' could be a gymnastic bar hooked across two others, a rope ladder strung out horizontally or simply a low bench between two large stage blocks. It must be a safe structure because some children are going to 'cross' the 'bridge' and it must be clearly visible to the rest of the children. A 'catching' adult should be on hand.

The children who 'cross' the 'bridge' should be barefoot or have on the footwear they use for movement. It will help if some of them are 'volunteers' who have never done this before but some of them should also be confident 'old-timers'. Crossing the bridge helps both them and the children who are watching to register ideas of precariousness and risk, of openness and trust.

This crossing exercise is an illustration of the song 'A Narrow Bridge' (on page 131): it could be a visual accompaniment to the singing or it could take place beforehand, allowing for the children who crossed to express what they felt when they wobbled, how they overcame fear, whether practice and experience really helped with their emotional state, whether having the adult nearby was reassuring or irritating!

The song can be sung in English, Hebrew or both: if time permits, it is effective to sing it in English after interviewing the 'crossers' and then, perhaps as a finale, to ask the crossers to cross again while singing in Hebrew. This reinforces the point of acquiring inner strength by moving from the familiar (English) to the unfamiliar (Hebrew). The song can be sung without the crossing exercise.

'A Narrow Bridge' is a Hebrew saying of an eighteenth/nineteenth-century Hasidic leader Rabbi Nachman of Bratzlav which is in the Ukraine. The melody is attributed to Baruch Hait and the English version is by Angela Wood.

This song says that going through life is a bit like wobbling on a bar (or bench) when you are scared you might fall off and get hurt. You have to be a bit scared because then you will be careful but if you were too scared you would never do anything at all! Close your eyes and imagine there's a deep river and the water is crashing against the stones or maybe there are dangerous creatures lurking in it and you have to cross a narrow bridge to get to the other side. What are you thinking? What are you feeling? Are you afraid of anything? What are you hoping for? How are you going to get to the other side? Are you saying anything to yourself?

Closing thought

The following statement could be recited collectively as a close to this assembly: it could also be used in every assembly on this theme so as to draw them together. It might help to have it written on a banner or poster, or projected overhead:

Being brave doesn't mean not being scared.
It means being scared but still going on.

The song

A Narrow Bridge

Slow and thoughtfully

This whole wide world we know   is a nar-row bridge,   is a nar-row bridge,
Kol   ha'-o-lam koo-lo,   ge-sher tzar m'-od,   ge-sher tzar m'-od,

is a nar-row bridge.   This whole wide world we know   is a nar-row bridge,
ge-sher tzar m'-od.   Kol   ha'-o-lam koo-lo,   ge-sher tzar m'-od,

Faster

is a nar-row bridge.   And what counts most is not to fear,   not to fear,
ge-sher tzar m'-od.   V'-ha'-i-kar,   v'-ha'-i-kar   lo l'-fa-hed,

Not to fear at all.   And what counts most is not to fear,   Not to fear at all.
Lo l'-fa-hed klal.   V'-ha'-i-kar,   v'-ha'-i-kar   Lo' l'-fa-hed   klal.

131

Mix and match

Book box

Shirley Hughes, *Dogger*, Picture Lions, 00 661464 7. A touching story of a girl's sacrificial, yet no-big-deal, love for her younger brother.

Jan Ormerod, *Be Brave, Billy*, Picture Lions, 1983, 0 00 662259 3. Dedicated to 'those parents and children who find it hard to be brave all the time', this book encourages the reader to reflect on what gives them a sense of risk or trust.

Vera Southgate, *The Elves and the Shoemaker*, Ladybird, 1965, 0 7214 0078 7. In this European folktale, the elves sacrifice much time and effort to help the shoemaker.

Naomi Lewis, *The Snow Queen*, Walker Books, 1988, 0 7445 0621 2. A fresh translation, poignantly illustrated, of the haunting story created by Hans Christian Andersen.

Cherry Denman, *The Little Peacock's Gift*, Picture Corgi Books, 1987, 0 552 52548 0. A gloriously illustrated version of this traditional story.

The video

Clip number 14 on the accompanying video cassette paints an inspiring and moving portrait of a twelve-year-old Welsh girl. Most of the children who previewed this video clip responded with silence. Later they wanted to talk and write about it at great length and also wanted to see it again. It was deeply important for many of them. Some said they felt proud of Caroline and wrote down what she said about life. This clip needs to be shown in a class or year-group setting where the children are with peers and adults whom they know quite well. There should be time immediately or soon afterwards for children to explore what they are feeling.

One night Caroline's house caught fire and she got out but realised that the baby was still inside so she ran back in to save him. Suddenly the house exploded and Caroline was caught in a fireball. The fire-fighters managed to rescue her but the baby was dead. Caroline spent a long time in hospital as she was very badly burned: all her mouth is scarred and she can't always speak very clearly. Everyone says she did something really brave but she is not big-headed about it. She loves playing football and just wants to be a normal kid. She says she would still do it again if she had to: it doesn't matter to her what she looks like and she just wants to get on with life.

To read out

If the group of children is small enough for the picture of the sheepdog to be clearly seen, it might be a good idea to introduce this extract through it and, especially for children who have no awareness of sheepfarming, to explain to them what sheepdogs do and what qualities they have.

Not only people can be brave: animals can be brave and they can give people a lot.

This is part of a story about a boy called David who had grown up in a concentration camp where people had been forced to go for no good reason and were treated very cruelly. One day David has the chance to escape and he runs away because he wants to find his family again. On his journey, some people are very kind and understanding and they look after him but even so he does not want to stay with them because he misses his own home, especially his mother. Then he is caught by a farmer who makes him work for nothing, hardly gives him anything to eat and locks him up at night. But there are two things that really help David: deep down inside, he believes that God will take care of him; he calls him 'God of the green pastures and still waters'. And he has a great friend, a dog called King and he gives David the best thing of all! Together they get away one night but they are soon followed by men in trucks who have big guns.

The dog kept nudging him. It wanted them to go back the way they had come, away from the spot where it sensed danger lurking.

'No,' David whispered, 'we can't go back – it's too late. You must keep still, King; and when they've hit me, perhaps you can get away by yourself.'

The dog licked his cheek eagerly, impatiently nudging him again and moving restlessly as if it wanted to get up. It nudged him once more – and then jumped up before David could stop it.

In one swift second David understood what the dog wanted. It did not run back the way they had come. It was a sheepdog and it had sensed danger. It was going to take David's place!

Barking loudly it sprang toward the men in the dark.

'Run!' something inside him told David. 'Run . . . run!' That was what the dog wanted him to do.

So he ran. He hesitated a moment and then ran more quickly than he had ever run in all his life. As he ran, he heard the men shouting and running too, but in a different direction . . . One of them yelled with pain – then came the sound of a shot and a strange loud bark from the dog.

David knew the dog was dead.

He went on running. He was some distance away now, and they had not heard him. But he ran on until he had left far behind the field where they had left the road an hour before. Then he threw himself down in a ditch sobbing, and gasping painfully for breath. ●

He felt as if he would never be able to stop crying, never. God of the pastures and waters . . . had let the dog run forward, although he knew it would be shot.

133

'Oh, you shouldn't have done it!' David sobbed again and again. 'The dog followed me, and I was never able to look after it properly. I couldn't even give it enough to eat and it had to steal to get food. The dog came with me of its own free will, and then had to die just because of it . . .'

But then David realised he was wrong. It was not because it had followed him that the dog was dead. The dog had gone with him freely, and it had met its death freely, in order to protect David from them. It was a sheepdog and it knew what it was doing. It had shown David what it wanted him to do, and then it had diverted the danger from him and faced it because it wanted to.

Its very bark as it sprang forward had seemed to say, 'Run, run!' And all the while David was running, he had known he must not turn back and try to save it. He must not let the dog's action be in vain: he had to accept it. So one could get something for nothing after all?

. . . .

(Ann Holm, *I Am David*, Magnet, 1965/86, 0 416 88470 9, pp. 185–7)

Elsewhere in the novel, David's name and his connection with the biblical David is explored: it was an adult inmate of the concentration camp who had told him about Psalm 23 and the God of the 'green pastures and still waters'. The meaning behind the story could be amplified most powerfully by reading or singing Psalm 23 in any one of its versions or renditions.

Many Christians see the dog's name 'King' as symbolic and his self-sacrifice as referring to the redemptive death of Jesus. This extract – and indeed this story – works particularly well in the fuller context of Easter reflections and celebrations.

. . . .

To read out

'The Peacock's Little Gift' is a Chinese folk tale of selfless love, appealing to children throughout the Primary years. The story is simple yet effective to retell or enact; peacock feathers or a picture of a peacock will help younger children especially to appreciate the story.

The peacocks in the forest wanted to learn some of the Peacock Fairy's power and mystery but she could not help all of them because they looked so much alike so she asked them to come back at midnight, looking different from one other. One little peacock who went away sad, feeling too ordinary to be chosen, met an old man who was burning up in the midday sun. He plucked out some of his feathers for a fan. Next he offered some feathers to a young woman to adorn her hair and her dress when she went to a dancing party. Then he gave some feathers to an old man who had to make a canopy for the Emperor's carriage and did not have the heart to kill peacocks. Finally, the peacock met a child who was sick in bed, longing for the Spring festival to come when there would be fireworks shooting through the air like peacock's feathers. But by then, the little peacock had no feathers left to give. ●

At midnight, all the other peacocks were preening themselves in silk and jewels – and the little peacock hardly looked like them at all. When the Peacock Fairy found out what had happened, she was so full of wonder and said she would make a firework display so alive with light and colour that the world would never forget it. So she plucked a feather from each of the other peacocks, waved her hand and the little peacock had a beautiful tail again. And when she whispered to him some special words to say to himself three times, his tail began to glow with fiery blue, green and purple as he soared through the air . . .

All these colours in the sky made the people cry out, 'The Spring Festival has begun!' And looking out from a lonely window to gaze upon the tail of firework feathers bursting over the world, the sick child was well again in a flash!

Closing thought

This prayer was specially written for *Assembly Kit* by the Rev. Peter Jenkins.

Dear God,

Sometimes you ask us to give up something we like so that other people can have it. More often people give up something *they* like so that we can have it. Some people, like Jesus, have even given up their *life* to help others.

Thank you for all the people who have given up something for us. Help us to be giving like them. Amen.

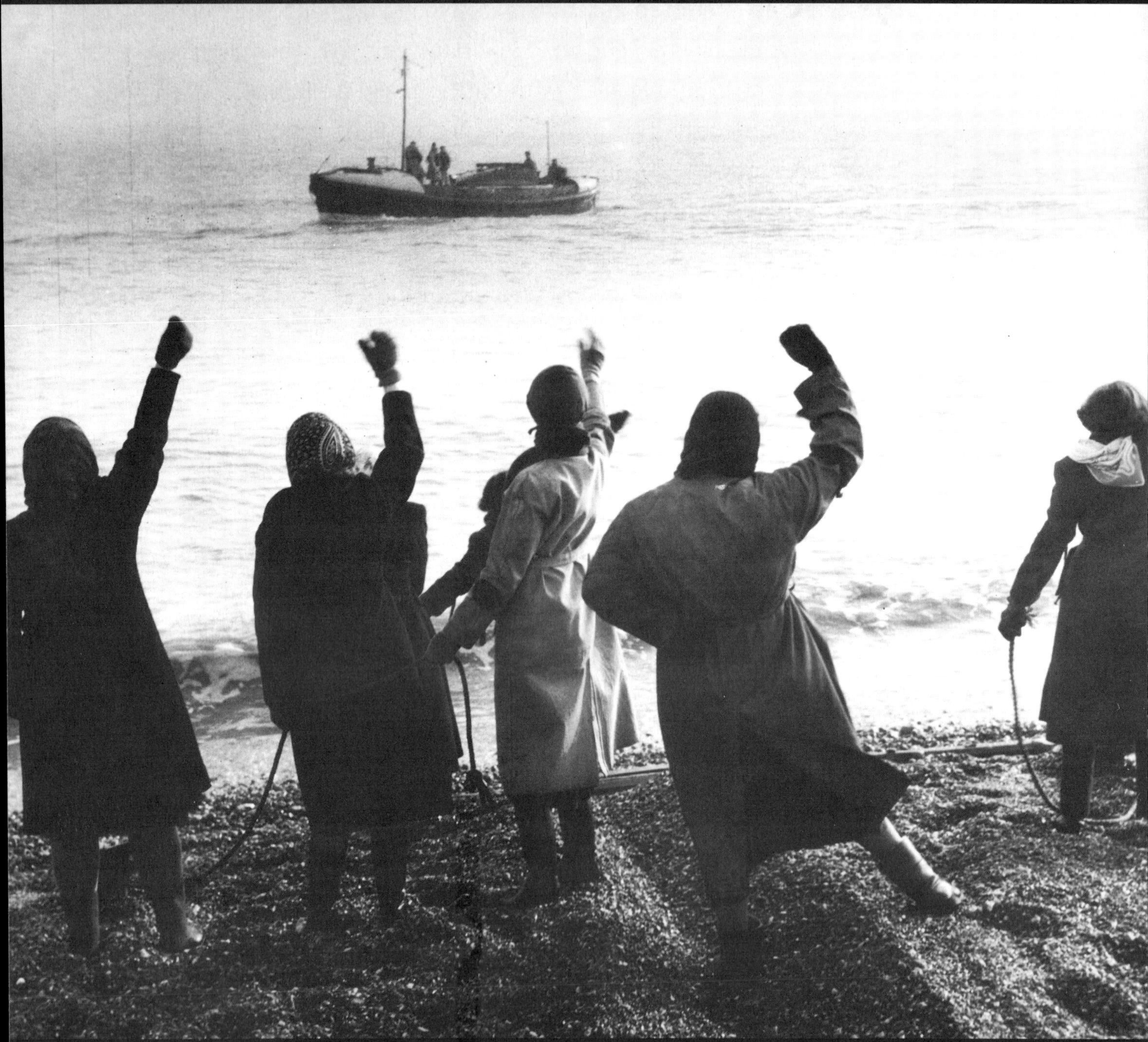

15

I'll miss you

Many teachers find the experience of death difficult to explore with children yet we know how much remembering helps healing and how important it is for people to be allowed to grieve. This process does not have to wait for an actual death, but can begin with a little loss in everyday experience.

losing, missing and dying

Children are likely to cope best with a particular experience of loss if they have opportunities over time to explore and reflect upon the wide range of losses and 'little deaths' which are a feature of everyday life. Yet in many schools talking about death is only occasioned by the actual decease of a person or animal. While this may be a 'crisis management' approach to children's bereavement, their mourning will be no less real and it might be comforting, educational and 'worshipful' for children to ritualise their grief together.

Frequently death gives no warning and one of the most difficult situations for any teacher to handle sensitively is the sudden demise of a class pet or a baby bird who fell from the nest . . . Some children will vocalise what should be 'done', while others may be too numb to speak or even think. Some may have been brought up in a religious tradition with significant beliefs about the afterlife and practices relating to the dead; some may have firm views of their own; and others may be overwhelmed or vague. Yet a decision to hold some form of funeral will inevitably be reached – whether suggested by the teacher, asserted by a strong-willed child, or emerging from group consensus.

An activity

One particularly moving and profound children's book provides a helpful structure for creating an activity of 'collective worship' involving an animal's funeral: Judith Viorst, *The Tenth Good Thing About Barney*, Collins, 1974, 0 00 195821 6. When a cat called Barney dies, a little boy is inconsolable and at bedtime his mother suggests that he think of ten things about Barney that he could say at the funeral in the morning. They bury the cat under a tree and the boy recites nine things, saying that he'll try to think of another later. A heated discussion with another child about whether Barney is in heaven or in the ground has to be settled by his father who says that no one knows for sure! Later, while planting seeds, the boy comes to understand that everything changes in the ground and that Barney will become part of the earth. That's the tenth good thing: Barney is 'helping to grow flowers . . . that's a pretty nice job for a cat'.

If a burial has been decided upon, tell or read the Barney story up to the point when the boy has to recite the 'ten good things'; then break off and ask the children, individually or in groups, to think of things they especially want to remember, and are grateful for, about the animal that has died. This will help to focus their grief, to heal by remembering and to learn the value of respecting the dead. Together, choose the *nine* 'things' that are most meaningful and let the children write a remembering scroll. Some children may want to read – or even compose – poems or prayers, while others will want to make a 'coffin', 'shroud' or gravestone.

At the funeral, tell or read the part of Barney's story about things changing in the ground. If it is seasonable and you have seeds or bulbs available, plant them as a symbol of the new life that the earth gives. Then let the children recite the *tenth* good thing . . .

Mix and match

The video

Clip number 15 on the accompanying video cassette depicts the disaster at the 1989 F.A Cup semi-final in Hillsborough which has had a deep and lasting effect on many of the young way beyond Liverpool, and looms large in national consciousness as an unspeakable tragedy. This news footage covers the scene of the disaster, of the spontaneous gifts of remembering love and of the memorial service later in Liverpool Cathedral. With thoughtful preparation, it can exemplify a grief that is powerfully expressed yet removed from children's usual expectations of bereavement and the immediate circumstances of their lives. *Previewing is strongly recommended.*

Football should be fun to play and to watch but once a match that was going to be really exciting turned out to be very sad. One of the Liverpool terraces got very crowded and more fans were coming in at the back, not knowing that the ones at the front were already squashed against the fence. Then people started pushing to get in and no one could get out. People in the stand above tried to pull others up but they couldn't reach many of them in time . . . and 95 supporters were crushed to death.

This film starts with fans trying to climb out of the terraces and with people running back and forth across the pitch with anything they can use as a stretcher to carry the wounded. No one seems ashamed to cry and to say what they feel. Before long, the terrace where the fans died is covered with fresh flowers from people who want to show how sad they are. Other fans tied their football club scarves to the railings as a sign that they belong together. Some time later, families and friends come to Liverpool Cathedral to remember the dead and to pray with each other. The Bishop asks God to give peace to the dead and strength to the ones who miss them.

. . . .

To read out

The Crush of Death

The Hillsborough ground was splattered with blood.

It was a rainy day with a field of mud.

This was the day when the people were crushed,

When the people wept and had to be hushed.

Along came the Bishop with his book of prayers.

They buried them then in muddy layers.

We saw the coffins; we saw the flags.

We saw the scarves and we saw the bags.

People were crying and people were dead.

And all I could do was lie on my bed!

(Jatinder Rahi, age 13)

Liverpool!

The crowd sang for their team.
The crowd cheered for their team.
The crowd screamed for their team.
The crowd cried for their team.
The crowd died for their team.

(Anju Pandhal, age 14)

Why Did It Happen?

Why did it happen? Was it God's way
Of telling us all that someone must pay?
Suffocation – they were all short of air!
Please stop a minute and show that we care.
If I could stop and change anywhere,
I'd change the Hillsborough day, I swear.

(Nicole Lewis, age 14)

Book box

Holly Keller, *Goodbye Max*, Walker, 1990, 0 7445 1455 X. Ben's dog Max was old and ill and died one day while he was at school. Ben is angry, incredulous and guilty, as well as sad.

Carol Curtis Stilz, *Kirsty's Kite*, Albatross, 1988, 0 86760 089 6. Kirsty's mother dies and she is left to the care of her grandfather.

Alice Walker, *To Hell with Dying*, Hodder and Stoughton, 1988, 0 340 430022 2. A tender and memorable book for older children from this celebrated woman writer of the Black American South.

Leo Buscaglia, *The Fall of Freddie the Leaf*, Holt, Rinehart and Winston, 1982, 0 03 062424 X. Aptly subtitled 'A Story of Life for all Ages' and illustrated with detailed colour photography of leaves, trees and parks, this parable traces the changes in a leaf through the passing seasons.

John Burningham's original story *Grandpa* (Picture Puffins, 1988, 0 14 050841 4), with its powerful picture of the empty armchair, was adapted for video and the 'book of the film' is now available with expanded text and additional illustrations.

The song

My Little Chick is Dead and Gone

This children's song in Tagalog comes from the Philippines. It was transmitted, transliterated and translated into English by Angela Wood. The music was transcribed by Walter Robson.

('Ang' has a long vowel, sounding between 'rung' and 'rang'. 'Ay' rhymes with 'pie'.)

Moderately

① My lit-tle chick is dead and gone!
   Ang ma-nok ko ay te - pok na!

② My lit-tle chick is dead and gone!
   Ang ma-nok ko ay te - pok na!

③ Cock-a-doo-dle-do! Doo-dle-do! Doo-dle-do!
   Ki-ree, ki-ree, koo! Ki-ree koo! Ki-ree koo!

④ My lit-tle chick is dead and gone!
   Ang ma-nok ko ay te - pok na!

To read out

These eleven-year-olds reflect on their experiences of loss:

'I get fed up when my next door neighbours' dog barks a lot: the other day he got lost, and they started to cry so I decided to look for him. At night, I was really worried and wished I had found him. But the next morning there was a dog barking at the front door – and it was him! Now I wish *I* had a dog!'
(Mukesh Bhudia)

'My parents had Calico before I was born and the first word I learned was "cat". She was so good-tempered. Suddenly she got ill and I stroked her a lot but in the end we had to have her put down. Mum cried. We brought Calico home and buried her in the garden under a calico bush which is very beautiful: she looked happy and peaceful and I was glad of that but I miss her. We have a cat-shaped tea cosy which looks almost like her. I wish it *was* her!'
(Rachel O'Connell)

'I was worried because the window was open and suddenly my bird flew out. I went looking for it and found a cat eating it so I scared it away. I buried my bird. I dug just a small hole in my garden and covered it up gently just in case he could feel the weight of the earth. I put stones all round it and a flower on the top.'
(Mario Pyne)

'I stared at his grave. Dead flowers lay beside it. I thought they had nine lives. This only had one – what went wrong?'
(Timmy Dorgu)

'There is one thing I will miss the very most. I don't know what that thing will be until it happens, but something I have had from the day I can remember is a very special feeling I have when I am with her.'
(Jemma Morphet)

'Tabatha has gone for ever
Like a part of me has died.
I couldn't work out why this happened
What she had done to deserve this
And who I was sad for
Her or me . . .'
(Rebecca Enorzah)

To read out

This extract contains a powerful experience of multiple loss. It will help the children to discuss why the Romany people traditionally burned all the deceased's belongings – what this betokened for their way of life before and after death . . . (If they are unable to read the rest of the book, they will be comforted to know that Kizzy and Joe slipped away that night and found a home of their own – and that Joe eventually died contented in an apple orchard.)

Kizzy lives with her Gran, their horse Joe and the travelling people – though she is only half-traveller, a 'diddakoi'. The night after Gran dies, Kizzy wakes up to find that her grandmother's wagon has been deliberately set on fire which makes her angry and upset. Although one of the traveller women is like an aunt to her, Kizzy begins to realise she doesn't really belong with the travellers any more but doesn't belong with any other people either. What do you think she'll do?

The fire seemed enormous and bright; it was the men trampling, not Joe. Kizzy stumbled to her feet and Mrs Smith caught her by the shoulders. 'It's all right, darlin'. You stay here with me,' but Kizzy was standing transfixed.

Flames were rushing up in the orchard, so bright they seemed to be dancing in the apple trees and so hot they seemed to scorch Kizzy's face. A trail of sparks streamed over the paddocks; it was as well that the young horses were in the stables at night . . .

Joe, like Kizzy, seemed transfixed. There was a smell of burning paint and wood and hot metal; the men walked round the great fire poking it with poles. They were burning the wagon; as Kizzy watched, the body sank, came away from the wheels and the roof fell in. 'But why?' asked Kizzy. 'Why?' ●

The words seemed to be wrung out of her, but they were quiet. Mrs Smith knelt down beside her and Kizzy smelt her comforting traveller smell, wood smoke and old clothes, but all the same she did not lean against Aunt Em. 'See, love, your Gran was an old-fashioned Romany and they, when they die, lays down that their wagon is to be burnt and all they things – yes, rightly, the china smashed up and ornaments and that – they clothes and photographs burned . . . your Gran wanted it and we promised.' She looked at Kizzy's face. 'Your Gran wanted it, sweetheart, so we had to do it.'

Gran's things: the bunks under the window, the lace curtains, the saucepans and bucket, the rag rug on the floor, Gran's chair, the table and shelves. Then – I can't live in the wagon, thought Kizzy. ▲

'And 'tisn't as if the wagon was any good; it's fallin' to pieces – no use to anyone, darlin'.'

'It was to me.' There was no use now in saying that.

'Never mind,' Mrs Smith's voice cut across her. 'You'll go to a nice house; nice clothes you'll have and good schooling. You'll end up like a lady,' and Mrs Smith put on her coaxing gypsy voice . . . but Kizzy was not listening. Panic had set in. 'What will happen to Joe?' asked Kizzy.

She asked that again, made herself ask it, when the flames had died down to smouldering red and they were once again having tea, sitting

144

round their own fire. 'But it's wunnerful warm everywhere,' said Mrs Smith. Only Kizzy was cold; even close to the fire she was shivering.

(Rumer Godden, *The Diddakoi*, Puffin, 1972/86, 0 14 030753 2, pp. 27–9)

To read out

My Grandad

I thought of him day by day;
I wonder why he couldn't stay.

But now I know, DEAD, gone forever.
I wish we could have been together.
Just perhaps for one more day
So I'd have a chance to say
How much I loved him.

(Karen Mfuk, age 11)

The cassette

'Spotty Harris', on the accompanying audio cassette, is a boy whose gerbil wins first prize in the school's best kept pet competition and then dies. This affects Spotty's relationship with his grandfather and makes him realise that he soon may also die. The story seems acted rather than read and a song on the theme that life goes on acts as a running motif.

Closing thoughts

God be in my head and in my understanding;
God be in my eyes and in my looking;
God be in my mouth and in my speaking;
God be in my heart and in my thinking;
God be at my end and at my departing.

(Sarum Primer, 16th century)

The flowers are finished. So is my song.
Accept my last offering, God.

(Rabindranath Tagore, classical Bengali poet)

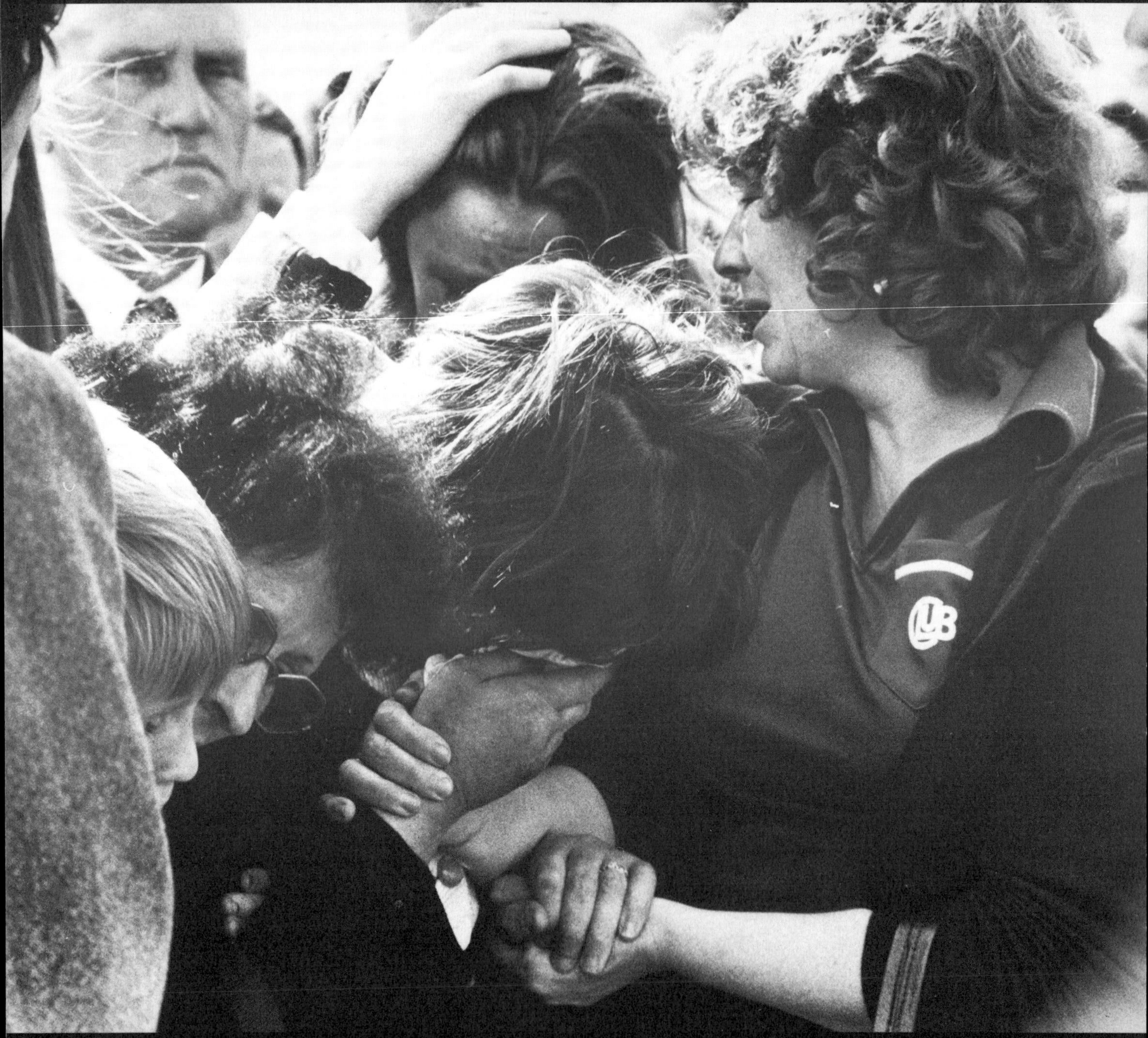
UB

16

I'm sorry - that's OK!

Being forgiven may be as difficult as forgiving, for the sense of hurt and regret can be intermingled. Self-forgiveness is perhaps hardest of all. The awareness that we have done something bad – and yet can be good – is central to a relationship with God and is a basic teaching in many faiths.

being hurt, saying sorry and forgiving

A spate of teasing and bullying may stimulate and necessitate an exploration of pain and repentance, or the themes might be generated for their own sake.

The video

Clip number 16 on the accompanying video cassette presents a convincing portrayal of tribal behaviour at school, the effects of teasing on an individual pupil, the comfort offered by peers and the growth in self-reflection by the main perpetrator. As well as a means of addressing the issue of bullying, this clip points to the need for acceptance, the capacity for forgiveness and an awareness of God in human life.

Some people like bullying and teasing other people unless they realise how horrid it is and how they would hate it to happen to them. In this play, some boys think it's clever to tease Edward for being posh, they love making people laugh at him and they feel big when they all gang up!

Some eight-year-old boys and girls reflected on the experience of being hurt and the dilemma involved in forgiving; their reflections are reproduced here anonymously. It is probably advisable, if using children as readers, to choose those to whom the circumstances described do *not* apply; and it is helpful to pause in silence after each reflection/testimony to allow for an empathetic response.

To read out

'If I was being bullied, you wouldn't know how I would feel! If I teased and bullied someone, I would feel sorry for them. I hope I could soon forgive myself and I hope they would soon forgive me.'

'They kick me and call me rude names which cannot be written. I feel outnumbered with a lot of bullies against me. Most of the time they come and say sorry and people like me are quite forgiving. I forgive them because I hope they won't do it again.'

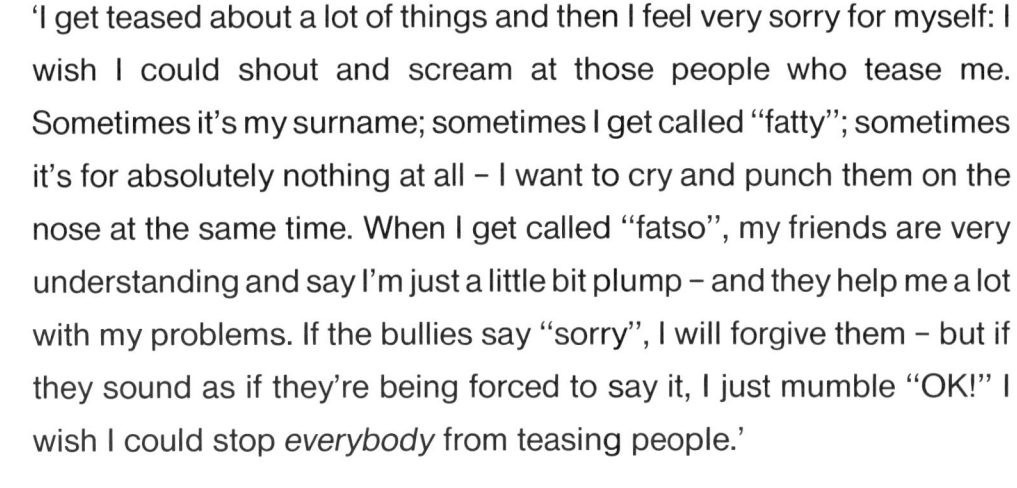

'I get teased about a lot of things and then I feel very sorry for myself: I wish I could shout and scream at those people who tease me. Sometimes it's my surname; sometimes I get called "fatty"; sometimes it's for absolutely nothing at all – I want to cry and punch them on the nose at the same time. When I get called "fatso", my friends are very understanding and say I'm just a little bit plump – and they help me a lot with my problems. If the bullies say "sorry", I will forgive them – but if they sound as if they're being forced to say it, I just mumble "OK!" I wish I could stop *everybody* from teasing people.'

'I get bullied because I wear silly clothes like my bicycle shorts just because they're black and pink and I feel embarrassed. When I am bullying someone, I don't really know what it feels like for the other person because they never told me. If I really did bully somebody, they might start to cry and then I would say sorry and feel forgiven. I'm really always sorry when I bully someone.'

'I like it when they say sorry and I can forgive them. That means I can trust them now.'

'When someone teases me about my smallness, it does not hurt me because I like being small; but when I'm teased about something I don't like, I get upset. I feel sorry when somebody gets into trouble because of me, when my teacher can't cope with the class or I did something wrong. It is a good thing to forgive – but still the other person shouldn't have done it!'

Closing thought

I didn't mean to be horrid and I'm not a horrid person. But I do feel horrid about what I did and about not saying that I'm sorry. I want to say, 'I'm sorry!' and it's so easy, really, yet the words won't come out. I know I'll feel better if I do and the longer I leave it the worse it will get. So maybe I'll just take a deep breath, smile and say from the bottom of my heart, 'I'm sorry, really I am!'

Mix and match

The song

Only one can talk at a time

This freshly composed song speaks of genuinely respecting others, of sharing insights and of giving everyone 'space':

The Punjabi and English words and the music were composed by Kulwant Wassu; the music was transcribed by Walter Robson.

Moderately

On-ly one can talk at a time And this is what I do: I lis-ten when you talk to me And then I talk to you!

In Punjabi

Briskly

Gal kar-i-yeh va-ro va-ree Teh eh'-heh meh'-ka-ra: Tu'-see gal eh'-ka-ro meh sun-di-ra, Teh per-e-meh gal eh'-ka-ra.

Book box

Hiawyn Oram, *Angry Arthur*, Picture Puffin, 1984, 0 14 050 426 5. A popular book with all ages, it graphically depicts a child's growing rage – and its consequences – for reasons long forgotten!

Susanna Gretz, *Joe Eats Bugs*, Beaver, 1990, 0 09 959740 3. Joe turns teasing into an experience of fun and growth.

Janet and Allan Ahlberg, *Burglar Bill*, Picture Lions, 1977, 0 00 661486 8. Through a delightfully 'hammy' plot and the key role played by a lost baby, Bill meets the woman of his dreams and sees the error of his ways.

Tomie de Paola, *Sing, Pierrot, Sing*, Harcourt Brace Jovanovich, 1983, 0 15 274989 6. A text-free book of vivid 'naïve' drawings.

Barrie Wade, *Little Monster*, Andre Deutsch, 1990, 0 233 98409 7. Big drawings and simple text tell of a black girl who hates her mother calling her 'as good as gold'.

Carol Olu Easmon, *Bisi and the Golden Disc*, Andre Deutsch, 1990, 0 233 98412 7. An original tale with authentic details of traditional Ghanaian life.

Angela Wood, 'Just a Drop', in *Faith Stories for Today*, BBC/Longman, 1990, 0 582 05946 1, pp. 34–9. A modernised Jewish folktale on the need to come to terms with oneself.

To read out

From a delightful collection about a black boy called Julian, this story explores children's experiences of temptation, guilt, and shame; and their loving father's humorous response which punishes, yet understands, and ultimately restores. For children who are unfamiliar with the cooking processes involved – which are crucial to understanding the twist of the story – it might be helpful to demonstrate a beater or whisk. A full appreciation of the story's subtlety is enhanced by intervening to ask the children what they anticipate will happen . . .

Julian and his younger brother Huey watch their father making their mother's favourite pudding as a special treat. He had to beat the egg yolks, whip the egg whites, squeeze the lemons, mix them together with sugar and cream, and let the whole thing cook until it bubbled. It looked and smelled so delicious that their mouths began to water. 'It will taste like a whole raft of lemons,' their father said. 'It will taste like a night on the sea.' He left the pudding on the counter in the kitchen to set, and told the boys to leave it alone!

But the pudding was so tempting that they kept picking at it until there was almost nothing left and they knew they'd done something wrong. So they ran into their bedroom, crawled under the bed and heard their father's deep voice booming all over the house.

'STAND UP!' he said . . . 'What do you have to tell me?'

'We went outside,' Huey said, 'and when we came back, the pudding was gone!'

'Then why were you hiding under the bed?' my father said. We didn't say anything. We looked at the floor. 'I can tell you one thing,' he said. 'There is going to be some beating here now! There is going to be some whipping!'

The curtains at the window were shaking. Huey was holding my hand. 'Go into the kitchen!' my father said, 'right now!' We went into the kitchen. 'Come here, Huey!' my father said. Huey walked towards him, his hands behind his back.

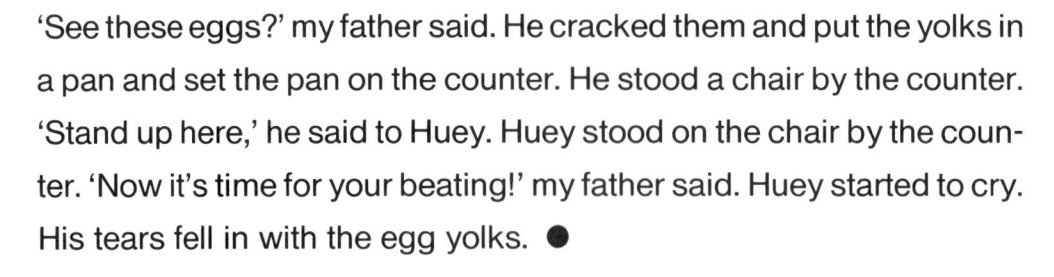

'See these eggs?' my father said. He cracked them and put the yolks in a pan and set the pan on the counter. He stood a chair by the counter. 'Stand up here,' he said to Huey. Huey stood on the chair by the counter. 'Now it's time for your beating!' my father said. Huey started to cry. His tears fell in with the egg yolks. ●

'Take this!' my father said. My father handed him the egg beater. 'Now beat those eggs,' he said. 'I want this to be a good beating!'

'Oh!' Huey said. He stopped crying and started to beat the egg yolks.

'Now you, Julian, stand here!' my father said.

I stood on a chair by the table. 'I hope you're ready for your whipping!' I didn't answer. I was afraid to say yes or no.

'Here!' he said, and he set the egg whites in front of me. 'I want these whipped and whipped well!'

'Yes, sir!' I said, and started whipping. My father watched us. My mother came into the kitchen and watched us. After a while, Huey said, 'This is hard work.'

'That's too bad,' my father said. 'Your beating's not done!' And he added sugar and cream and lemon juice to Huey's pan and put the pan on the stove. And Huey went on beating.

'My arm hurts from whipping,' I said.

'That's too bad,' my father said. 'Your whipping's not done.' So I whipped and whipped, and Huey beat and beat. 'Hold that beater in the air, Huey!' my father said. Huey held it in the air. ▲

'See!' my father said. 'A good beating stays on the beater. It's thick enough now. Your beating's done.' Then he turned to me. 'Let's see those egg whites, Julian!' he said. They were puffed up and fluffy. 'Congratulations, Julian!' he said. 'Your whipping's done!'

He mixed the egg whites into the pudding himself. Then he passed the pudding to my mother. 'A wonderful pudding,' she said. 'Would you like some, boys?'

'No thank you,' we said.

She picked up a spoon. 'Why, this tastes like a whole raft of lemons,' she said. 'This tastes like a night on the sea.'

(Ann Cameron, 'The Pudding Like a Night on the Sea', in *Stories Round the World*, Hodder and Stoughton, 1990, 0 340 51270 9, pp. 44–6; originally published by A. P. Watt Ltd and Victor Gollancz Ltd)

Closing thought

A Christian prison chaplain encouraged young offenders in America to talk about their experiences of life and their feelings about themselves. Gradually they began to speak about God and to express their beliefs in poetry and prose.

This litany is effective if it is read responsively by *volunteers*: children may wish to create their own, mirroring this form; but if they are to be read out, the children's *privacy* must be protected. It is therefore prudent to suggest to the pupils that they create a litany for a *historical* or *fictional* character they know.

That we don't think much about you
We is sorry, God.
That we used your name wrong
We is sorry, God.
That we make believe we don't care about you
We is sorry, God.
That we think it's big stuff to do
We is sorry, God.
That we poke fun at people who go to church
We is sorry, God.
That we done it so much
We is sorry, God.

That we waited so long to say we is sorry
We is sorry, God.
That we hate your mercy
We is sorry, God.
That we forget your love
We is sorry, God.

For being too big
We is sorry, God.
For not findin' out about you
We is sorry, God.
For fightin' you
We is sorry, God.
For being tough about you
We is sorry, God.
For thinkin' we is all alone
We is sorry, God.

For all the times we said, 'Who needs God?'
We is sorry, God.
For all that kinda stuff
We is sorry, God.

(Carl Burk, *Treat Me Cool, Lord*, Fontana, 1969, 62ff)

東海道五拾三次之内 小田原 酒匂川

廣重画

17

The real me

The pressure to conform can be very convincing, yet each of us is unique and can discover what is special about ourselves, and live with integrity.

uniqueness and integrity

The video

Clip number 17 on the accompanying video cassette captures the famous events of Tiananmen Square, Beijing, in the spring of 1989. It has become one of the landmarks in modern history and holds a brief yet memorable vision of the power of a single individual – the one against the many. The political issues may at first seem too complicated for Primary children but the sheer visual impact of the student's action powerfully transcends that particular situation. Though the reporter comments, 'A lone figure made one last hopeless gesture' and though it was undoubtedly unsuccessful in immediate terms, yet it offers us all a symbol of spiritual resistance.

For many years, the government of China said what people should learn at school or college and they only let them have certain kinds of books or films. They were not allowed to ask their teachers real questions or find things out for themselves. They heard there were students in other countries who could learn all kinds of things, could find out about life however they liked and could make up their own minds. Chinese students wanted to be free like that but the government refused. To show they really meant what they said, the students pitched tents in a square in the city and wouldn't move unless things got better; they burned the Chinese flag to show how cross they were; they sang songs about freedom; they made a model of the American 'Statue of Liberty', which is a sign of freedom, and put it up facing a picture of a very famous leader called Mao. The government were so angry they sent in the army which chased the students away and even killed some of them.

Then something amazing happened: with his arms in the air, a student stepped right in front of a line of tanks that was coming across the square. The front tank swerved a bit and the student stepped in front again. The tank dodged and the student moved in front a third time. That student became quite famous though we do not know his name. We do not even know what happened to him in the end. But we do know that he was on his own and very small, yet he could make a mighty tank move.

To read out

Karmit Grewal, age 14, wrote a poem about that student, as though from his point of view:

No Through Way!

No through way,
Run me over,
Blow me away,
You can't go around,
Unless you knock me down,
No matter what you say,
No through way,
Run me over,
Blow me away,
No through way!

I feel anger,
I feel sad,
Leave the students alone,
Give them what they want,
And should already have.
No through way,
Run me over,
Blow me away!

I won't let you through,
No matter what you do,
No matter what you say,
No through way,
Run me over,
Blow me away,
No . . . through . . . way!

To read out

For many years, people in Britain have felt that the government was not giving enough or doing enough for the hospitals, doctors, nurses and others like the ambulance workers. In 1990 ambulance workers tried lots of ways to make things better and to be able to look after the patients properly, and they wanted everybody to know about it. Their supporters called a 15-minute stand-up one lunch-time so that everybody could see how much support there was. This is what happened to two 11-year-olds:

To read out

'I stood up at lunch-time for 15 minutes. This made it hard to eat but I felt strongly about supporting the ambulance workers.'
(Joey Coker)

'When I got into the canteen, a dinner lady said, "Sit down!" but I didn't. She took me to the Headteacher and I told her that I was standing up for the ambulance dispute . . . You should always stand up for your beliefs.'
(Jason Jenn)

Closing thought

With some unpacking of meaning, this statement will draw the ideas together for the children and could be boldly displayed:

*'If you don't stand for something,
You'll fall for anything!'*

Mix and match

To read out

Alice

She drank from a bottle called DRINK ME
And up she grew so tall,
She ate from a plate called TASTE ME
And down she shrank so small.
And so she changed, while other folks
Never tried nothin' at all.

(Shel Silverstein, *Where the Sidewalk Ends*, Harper and Row, 1974, p. 112)

To read out

Alice is sitting on the grass with her older sister on a warm afternoon but is bored with the book she is reading and falls asleep. In her dream, she falls down a rabbit hole and drinks from a bottle which says 'Drink me!' – and suddenly starts to change size! Soon after that she meets a caterpillar.

'Who are *you*?' said the Caterpillar . . .

Alice replied, rather shyly, 'I – I hardly know, sir, just at present – at least, I know who I *was* when I got up this morning, but I think I must have changed several times since then.'

'What do you mean by that?' said the Caterpillar sternly. 'Explain yourself!'

'I can't explain *myself*, I'm afraid, sir,' said Alice, 'because I'm not myself, you see.'

'I don't see,' said the Caterpillar. ●

'I'm afraid I can't put it more clearly,' Alice replied very politely, 'for I can't understand it myself to begin with; and being so many different sizes in a day is very confusing.'

'It isn't,' said the Caterpillar.

'Well, perhaps you haven't found it so yet,' said Alice; 'but when you have to turn into a chrysalis – you will some day, you know – and then after that into a butterfly, I should think you'll feel it a little queer, won't you?'

'Not a bit,' said the Caterpillar.

'Well, perhaps your feelings may be different,' said Alice; 'all I know is, it would feel very queer to *me*.' ▲

'You!' said the Caterpillar contemptuously. 'Who are *you*?'

Which brought them back to the beginning of the conversation. Alice felt a little irritated . . . and she drew herself up and said, very gravely, 'I think you ought to tell me who *you* are, first.'

'Why?' said the Caterpillar.

. . . Alice could not think of any good reason, and as the Caterpillar seemed to be in a *very* unpleasant state of mind, she turned away.

'Come back!' the Caterpillar called after her. 'I've something important to say . . . So you think you're changed, do you?' ■

'I'm afraid I am, sir,' said Alice; 'I can't remember things as I used – and I don't keep the same size for ten minutes together!' . . .

'What size do you want to be?' it asked.

'Oh, I'm not particular as to size,' Alice hastily replied; 'only one doesn't like changing so often, you know.'

(Lewis Carroll, *Alice's Adventures in Wonderland*, Dean and Son, 1974, pp. 36–8)

An activity

See how – or if – the children solve this . . .

A Chinese thinker once dreamed that he was a butterfly and when he woke up, he wondered: am I a man who dreamed I was a butterfly or am I really a butterfly who is now dreaming that he is a man?

The cassette

The story 'Chameleon' on the accompanying audio cassette concerns the irritation and insecurity a chameleon causes many animals, through being able to change colour. The chameleon points out that changeability is constant and that anyway other animals change *moods*!

Activities

With a sense of wonder, Jesus spoke of God as having counted the hairs on our heads. Allow the children a few minutes to *begin* to count their hair: they may well be overcome with amazement that they have been counting for so long and have only counted just a lock of hair!

For this midrash (Jewish 'explaining story') it is useful to have a few coins of the same denomination: some of the children near you could be shown the monarch's head and asked whether the coins are the same or different.

A king or queen creates their image on a coin – and it is always exactly the same.

But God creates us in his own image – and no two of us are ever alike!

Book box

Mwenye Hadithi, *Crafty Chameleon*, Picture Knight, 1987, 0 340 48698 8. Tired of being bothered and threatened, a chameleon devises a clever plan.

Leo Lionni, 'Fish is Fish', in *Frederick's Tales*, Andersen Press, 1986, 0 8666264 140 3, pp. 23–32 (also available separately). A tadpole and a tiny minnow are friends but the tadpole soon becomes a frog, hops out of the pond and experiences many new things.

John Agard, *Lend Me Your Wings*, Picture Knight, 1988, 0 340 48695 3. Sister Fish and Brother Bird swap fins and wings so as to explore each other's worlds.

Tricia Tusa, *Chicken*, Macdonald, 1987, 0 356 13509 8. Being a chicken does not have to make you 'chicken'.

Anthea Bell (trans.), *The Nightingale*, Picture Book Studio, 1984, 0 907234 57 7. An accessible modern translation of this touching story by Hans Christian Andersen.

Janice Schoop, *Boys Don't Knit*, Women's Press, 1986, 0 88961 107 6. Discovering that his friend's grandfather unashamedly enjoys knitting, a boy's appreciation of his grandfather's craft – and his own self-image – are deepened and enlarged.

Margaret Mahy, *The Boy with Two Shadows*, Picture Lions, 1989, 0 00 663070 7. A boy wants to look after his shadow because it's the only one he's got.

To read out

It helps the children to focus on the meaning of this poem if the reader pauses at the end of the first line of each couplet and the listeners are asked to imagine . . . and perhaps even articulate – what does lie beneath . . .

Beneath the Surface

Beneath the surface of the water
There are fish, whales and dolphins.

Beneath the surface of the earth
There are worms, moles and rabbits.

Beneath the surface of your skin
There are bones, veins and muscles.

Beneath the surface of a quilt
There is a teddy, sheets and a hot water bottle.

Beneath the surface of my mind
There is winning, thinking and working.

(Johnathen McKay, age 9, in The Dyslexia Institute (ed.), *As I See It*, Walker Books, 1990, 0 7445 1601 3, p. 20)

To read out

An airplane has to crash-land in the desert and, when the pilot gets out, he meets 'The Little Prince', who tells him what his planet is like, how he feels about living things and how he came to see that the rose he cared for was truly special.

'Who are you?' he demanded, thunderstruck.

'We are roses,' the roses said.

And he was overcome with sadness. His flower had told him that she was the only one of her kind in all the universe. And here were five thousand of them, all alike, in one single garden! . . . 'I thought that I was rich, with a flower that was unique in all the world; and all I had was a common rose . . .' and he lay down in the grass and cried.

It was then that the fox appeared . . .

'Who are you?' asked the little prince, and added, 'You are very pretty to look at.'

'I am a fox,' the fox said.

'Come and play with me,' proposed the little prince. 'I am so unhappy.'

'I cannot play with you,' the fox said. 'I am not tamed. . . .'

'What does that mean – "tame"? . . .'

'It means to establish ties . . . To me, you are still nothing more than a little boy who is just like a hundred thousand other little boys. And I have no need of you. And you, on your part, have no need of me. To you, I am nothing more than a fox like a hundred thousand other foxes. But if you tame me, then we shall need each other. To me, you will be unique in all the world. To you, I shall be unique in all the world . . .'

'There is a flower . . . I think that she has tamed me . . .' ●

The little prince went away, to look again at the roses. 'You are not at all like my rose,' he said. 'As yet you are nothing. No one has tamed you, and you have tamed no one. You are like my fox when I first knew him. He was only a fox like a hundred thousand other foxes. But I have made him my friend, and now he is unique in all the world . . . In herself alone my rose is more important than all the hundreds of you other roses: because it is she that I have watered; because it is she that I have put under the glass globe; because it is she that I have sheltered behind the screen; because it is for her that I have killed the caterpillars . . . ; because it is she that I have listened to, when she grumbled, or boasted, or even sometimes when she said nothing. Because she is *my* rose . . .'

'Goodbye,' said the fox. 'And now here is my secret, a very simple secret: It is only with the heart that one can see rightly; what is essential is invisible to the eye... It is the time you have wasted for your rose that makes your rose so important... You become responsible, forever, for what you have tamed...'

(Antoine de Saint-Exupery, *The Little Prince*, Pan Books, 1945/75, 0 330 23945 7, pp. 62, 64ff, 70f)

Closing thoughts

This is very effective if recited collectively or boldly displayed:

There is only one me.

This traditional prayer of the Tewa people of North America evokes the idea of people as unique yet interdependent; warp and weft will need explanation/demonstration:

O our Mother the Earth, O our Father the Sky,
Your children are we, and with tired backs
We bring you the gifts of love.
Then weave for us a garment of brightness;
May the warp be the bright light of morning,
May the weft be the red light of evening,
May the fringes be the falling rain,
May the border be the standing rainbow.
Thus weave for us a garment of brightness,
That we may walk fittingly where birds sing,
That we may walk fittingly where grass is green,
O our Mother the Earth, O our Father the Sky.

A teaching from the Buddhist text, the Dhammapada:

'Whatever we are is because of what we thought.

'If we think bad things when we speak or act, unhappiness will follow us just like the cart follows the ox. Then we will be unhappy.

'If we think good things when we speak or act, happiness will follow us like a shadow. Then we will be happy.'

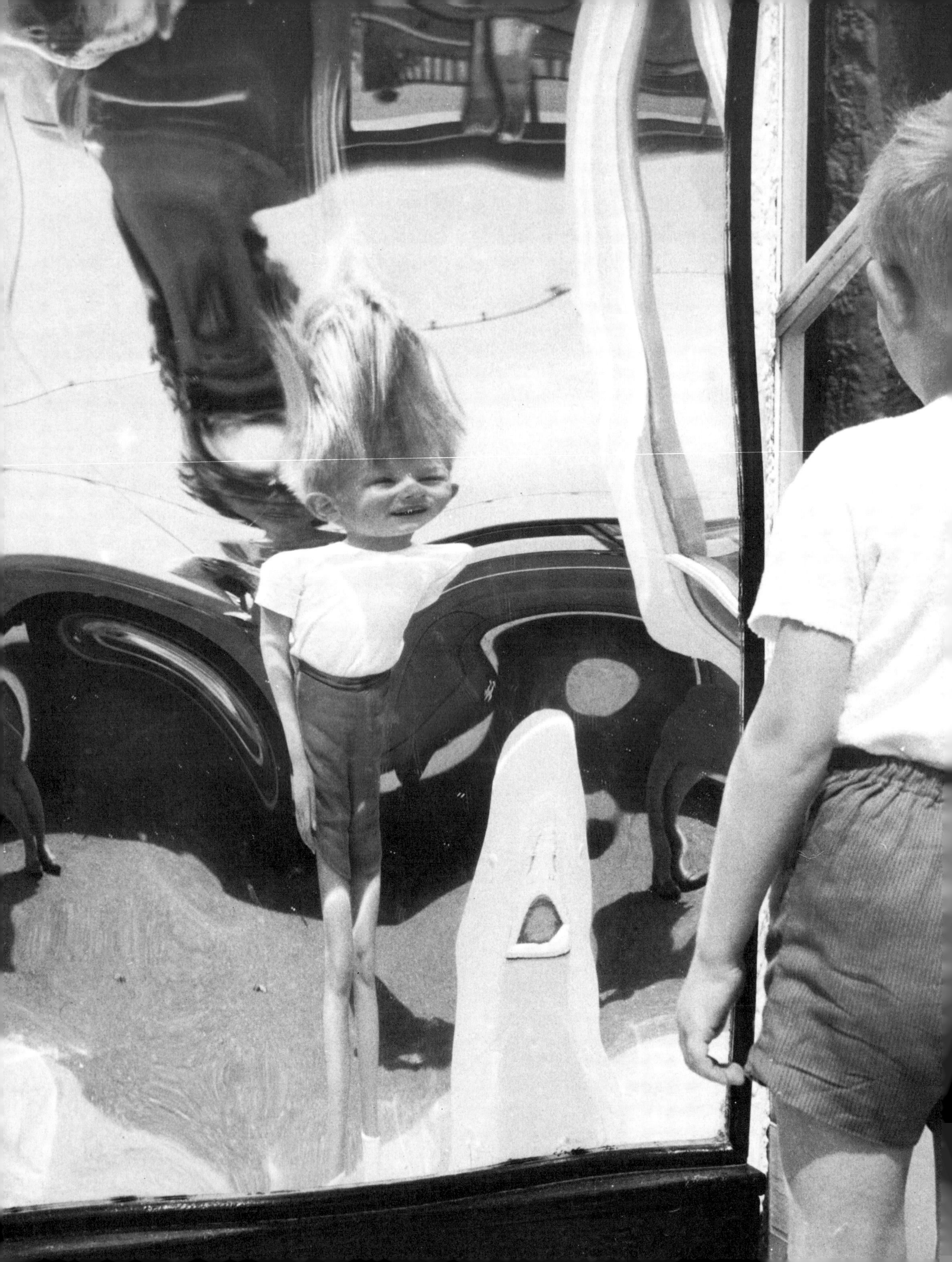

18
Me and my body

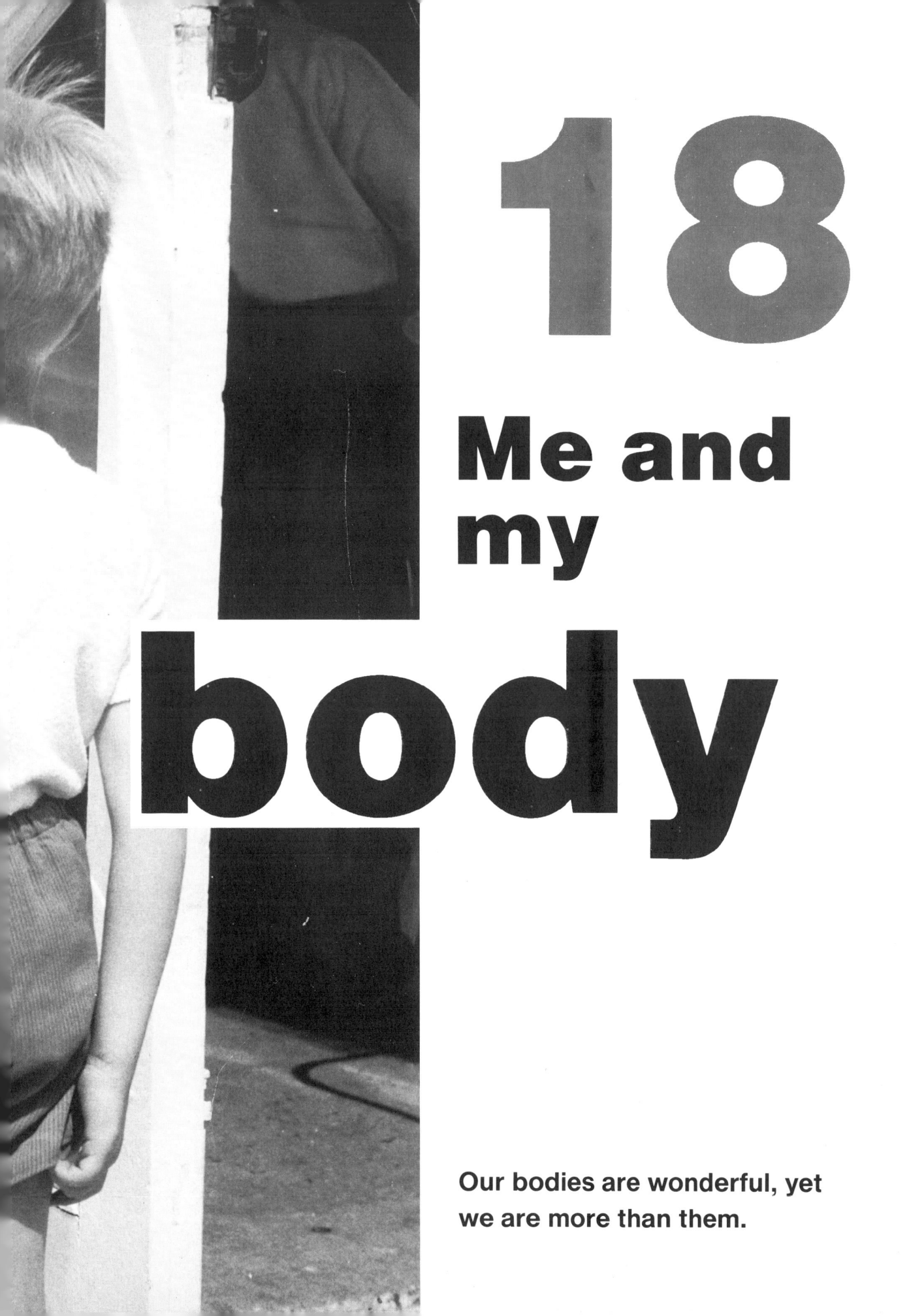

Our bodies are wonderful, yet we are more than them.

senses and appearances

To read out

In this American poem, a child says that our bodies are special and come from God, but mothers make up rules which stop us enjoying lots of things in life!

Ma and God

God gave us fingers – Ma says, 'Use your fork.'
God gave us voices – Ma says, 'Don't scream.'
Ma says eat broccoli, cereal and carrots.
But God gave us tasteys for maple ice cream.

God gave us fingers – Ma says, 'Use your hanky.'
God gave us puddles – Ma says, 'Don't splash.'
Ma says, 'Be quiet, your father is sleeping.'
But God gave us garbage can covers to crash.

God gave us fingers – Ma says, 'Put your gloves on.'
God gave us raindrops – Ma says, 'Don't get wet.'
Ma says be careful, and don't get too near to
Those strange lovely dogs that God gave us to pet.

God gave us fingers – Ma says, 'Go wash 'em.'
But God gave us coal bins and nice dirty bodies.

The song

My Body

This traditional Gujarati song expresses appreciation for the wonder of the human body – its awareness, its power and its sensitivity. It is especially appropriate for young children who will readily express the meaning of each verse in actions.

The song was transmitted and transliterated by Kanta Gomez; the music was transcribed by Keith Lovell; and the English version was written by Angela Wood.

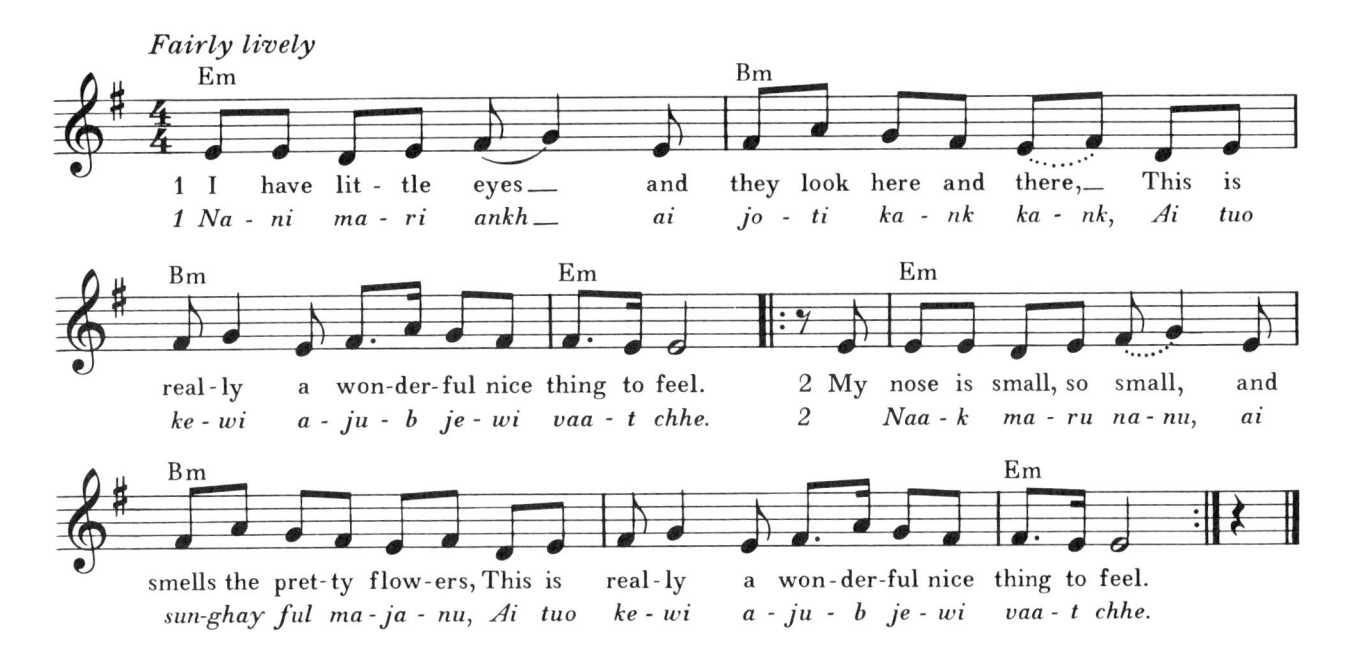

Fairly lively

1. I have little eyes and they look here and there, This is really a wonderful nice thing to feel.
1. Na - ni ma - ri ankh ai jo - ti ka - nk ka - nk, Ai tuo ke - wi a - ju - b je - wi vaa - t chhe.

2. My nose is small, so small, and smells the pretty flowers, This is really a wonderful nice thing to feel.
2. Naa - k ma - ru na - nu, ai sun - ghay ful ma - ja - nu, Ai tuo ke - wi a - ju - b je - wi vaa - t chhe.

3. My ears are small, so small and they hear things that matter . . .
   Nana mara kaan ai sambhade dai dhyan . . .

4. My mouth is small, so small and always speaks with kindness . . .
   Nanu maru modhu ai bhole saru saru . . .

5. My hands are small, so small and seven times I clap them . . .
   Nana mara hath ai tadhi pade saath . . .

6. My feet are small, so small and tiptoe round about you . . .
   Pug mara nana ai chale chhana mana . . .

Mix and match

Activities

Simple exercises can introduce the fact that our senses can deceive us and that things are not always what they seem:

Wrap the cover of a really popular book in brown paper: ask the children what sort of book they think it is.

If orange juice is delivered in milk bottles in your area, hide a bottle of orange juice then show the children an empty bottle and ask them what came in it. Surprise them with the juice!

'Walking my friend' has been used in some Primary schools for many years but its origin may be unknown: it increases self-awareness as well as empathy. Two children leave the others and take turns to watch each other walking. They then practise one of their walks they could *both* do and return to the group, walking *together*. The others guess whose walk they are walking!

Perhaps try again the egg tricks from Assembly 1, p. 12.

'Poppies' are cuddly toys which look like soft balls yet, when turned inside out, reveal a strange creature. (They are made by 'Those Characters' in Cleveland, USA, and are available in Britain.) Through them, children can explore the idea that they have an inner self which only sometimes shows – if at all. They might talk about this with someone they trust or present the ideas in art, such as by placing one piece of paper over another and attaching them along one side. On the top sheet, they could draw the way they think that other people see them and on the bottom sheet the way they see themselves – revealed only by lifting the flap . . .

Matrushka ('Mother Russia') dolls are made of brightly painted wood. They vary in size from a peanut to a poodle. Precisely crafted in small gradations, one doll will fit snugly into the next – with perhaps up to twenty dolls. Traditionally, Matrushka symbolised motherhood, which carries within an infinite number of generations, yet Soviet dissidents have given her a new interpretation: their children grow up in a difficult double-existence for they live *in* the State yet are not *of* the State. Parents and children playing together with Matrushka have something tangible to help them think through the layers of meaning in their lives. While our children's situation may not be so dramatic, a Matrushka doll can help them think through their roles and self-images.

The video

Clip number 18 on the accompanying video cassette makes us aware of the enormous sensitivity of the animal world – a truly humbling experience. Children will be helped by identifying the five senses we have and reminding themselves of their value.

We sometimes think we're the cleverest creatures in the world. We have five senses which tell us things but animals can sense a lot that we can't. Birds can see and hear many things we don't even know are there . . . goldfish can see colours that are invisible to us . . . dogs are a million times better at smelling than we are . . . there are many things we can't taste . . . and even if we feel a mosquito on our skin we don't hear or see all it can . . .

Some people say they have a sixth sense, that they somehow know things without their five senses. Perhaps we all have a sixth sense! What do you think?

To read out or act

The Effendi is a wise and witty folk hero of the Uygur people of China. Legends spread throughout Asia and the Middle East, where he is known as Nasrudin (pronounced 'Nass-er-deen'). This story is fun to enact.

168

The Effendi went to a big party wearing his shabbiest clothes. This embarrassed the host in front of the other guests and he reluctantly asked him to leave.

The Effendi thought that it didn't matter what someone wears and that it's the person that counts but if the host wanted everyone to dress up, then he would. So he put on his best suit and went back to the party. The host was so relieved to see the Effendi in nice clothes that he asked him to take a place of honour at the top table.

When the meal was served, the Effendi shocked everyone by standing up and dipping his clothes into the food. '*You* have been invited!' he said to his suit, 'so eat!'

To read out

This story of nursery magic easily adapts as a dialogue.

'What is REAL?' asked the Rabbit one day . . . 'Does it mean having things that buzz inside you and a stick-out handle?'

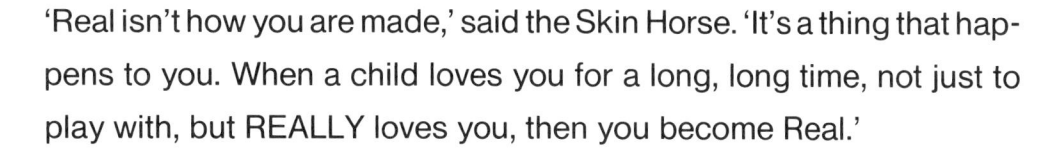

'Real isn't how you are made,' said the Skin Horse. 'It's a thing that happens to you. When a child loves you for a long, long time, not just to play with, but REALLY loves you, then you become Real.'

'Does it hurt?' asked the Rabbit.

'Sometimes,' said the Skin Horse, for he was always truthful. 'When you are Real you don't mind being hurt.'

'Does it happen all at once, like being wound up,' he asked, 'or bit by bit?' ●

'It doesn't happen all at once,' said the Skin Horse. 'You become. That's why it doesn't often happen to people who break easily, or have sharp edges, or who have to be carefully kept. Generally, by the time you are Real, most of your hair has been loved off, and your eyes drop out and you get loose in the joints and very shabby. But these things don't matter at all, because once you are Real you can't be ugly, except to people who don't understand.'

'I suppose *you* are Real?' said the Rabbit. And then he wished he had not said it, for he thought the Skin Horse might be sensitive. But the Skin Horse only smiled.

'The Boy's Uncle made me Real,' he said. 'That was a great many years ago; but once you are Real you can't become unreal again. It lasts for always.'

(Margery Williams, *The Velveteen Rabbit*, Doubleday, 1970, pp. 16–20)

To read out

Hands are for eating;
Hands are for beating.

Hands are for lighting a fire;
Hands are for waving higher and higher.

Hands are for wearing gloves;
Hands are for holding doves.

(Ester Gluck, age 7)

Book box

Mary Hoffman and Joanna Burroughes, *My Grandma has Black Hair*, Beaver, 1988, 0 09 957420. A grandmother challenges stereotypes and defies conventions, and likes to be called 'Sylvia'.

John Burningham, *Avocado Baby*, Fontana, 1982, 0 00 662591 6. A baby fails to thrive until siblings suggest feeding it avocado!

Anthony Browne, *Willy the Wimp*, Magnet, 1986, 0 416 53230 6. Puny and timid, Willy hates his nickname so decides on a special diet and a range of exercises.

Babette Cole, *Nungi and the Crocodile*, Macmillan, 1982, 0 333 39360 0. A crocodile falls blindly in love with an ostrich and has to be taught the lesson that crocodiles belong with crocodiles and ostriches belong with ostriches . . .

Miyoko Matsutani, *The Crane's Reward*, A. & C. Black, 1983, 0 7136 2335 7. This Japanese story tells how a poor elderly couple rescued a trapped crane and sheltered a homeless young woman.

Leo Lionni, 'Tico and the Golden Wings', in *Frederick's Tales*, Andersen Press, 0 86264 140 3, pp. 63–72. Teased by other birds for having golden wings, Tico gives away feathers one by one to people in need of gold.

Lynne Bradbury, *The Ugly Duckling*, Ladybird, 1979, 0 7214 0588 6. The well-loved Hans Christian Andersen story 'retold for easy reading'.

Rani and Jugnu Singh, 'The Donkey and the Tiger Skin', in *Stories from the Sikh World*, Macdonald, 0 356 13165 3, pp. 34–7. Guru Gobind Singh places on a donkey's back a tiger skin which he had received as a gift.

Angela Wood, 'Inside Out', in *Faith Stories for Today*, BBC/Longman, 1990, 0 582 05946 1, pp. 10–15. Returning from hajj in Mecca, a cat *seems* transformed into a devout Muslim but pounces on a mouse!

Closing thoughts

'If I could choose a sixth sense, I would look into the future because if something really bad was going to happen to me I would be able to change it. If my Mum and I were about to cross the road and if my Mum was going to get run over, I could somehow stop her. I would find it very difficult to cope with if someone in my family died. That's why I would choose this as my sixth sense.'

(Dan Selby Plewman, age 11)

'Lord, I can run and jump and shout and SING!
I can skip and clap and stamp and SWING!
Thank you for making me alive!'

(St Saviour's Priory, in Louise Carpenter (ed.), *The Puffin Book of Prayers*, 1990, 0 14 034348 2, p. 15)

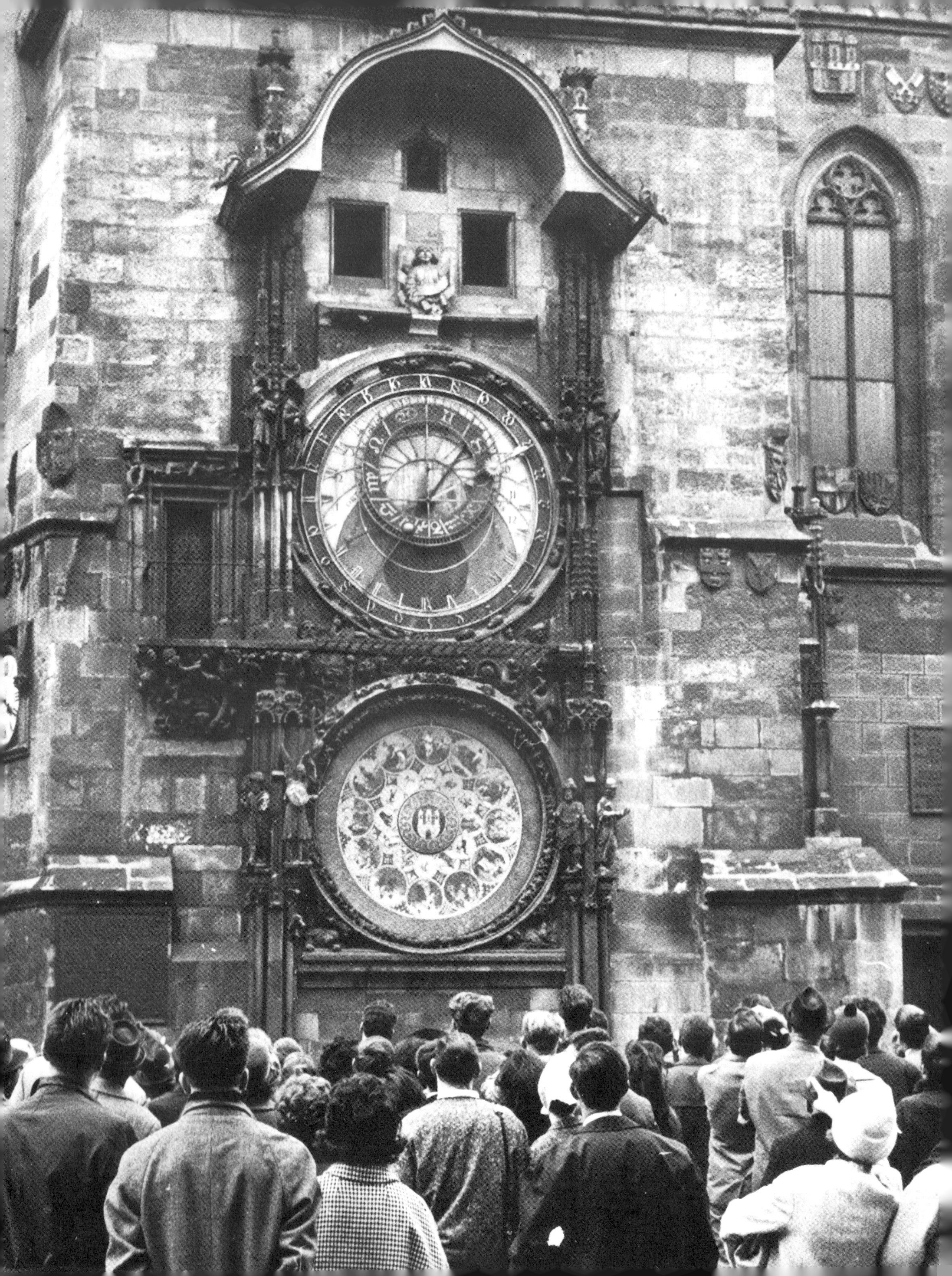

19
Tick!
tock!

Time is relative and elusive: paradoxically human societies have always sought both to measure time and to suggest that it is infinite . . . and festivals point to both these aspects.

time

An activity

Have a whistle and a stopwatch (or large clock with a second hand that is clearly visible). Ask a few children to work with you as time-keepers and callers/blowers and agree on a *precise* amount of time for this double experiment (one minute for each part is probably the right amount) – but keep that a secret from the other children! Invite the children to run around (or, if space does not permit, to jump up and down on the spot) and make as much noise as they like! When the time is up, but without telling the children how long has passed, blow the whistle and then ask them to sit down quietly, and stay *absolutely* silent and still. After the *same* length of time, blow the whistle again. Then invite the children to say which exercise lasted longer: older children could reasonably be asked to estimate the length of time each took. Invariably, sitting still and quiet seems to drag while gay abandon seems to fly! The 'witnesses' can then reveal that the two were identical and the others could speculate why they seemed different. It is important to point out to the children that they were not actually stupid if they didn't realise the two activities took the same time and that time *does* pass differently for different people and in different situations. A discussion could ensue on the need to have common time measurements.

This could lead fruitfully to an exploration of the many units in which people measure time (seconds, minutes, hours, days, weeks, months, years . . .); how they record time (timers, school bell, diaries, calendars, year-books . . .); and the reasons why religious traditions mark time, turning ordinary moments into special occasions (daily cycles of prayers, days of rest, annual festivals of celebration and commemoration . . .).

The video

The treatment of the relativity of time (in clip number 19 on the accompanying video cassette) is absolutely captivating yet difficult to comprehend at first: children may need to see it more than once and to have variations in speed pointed out.

When we move, we seem fast to a slow animal and slow to a fast animal. Have you ever wondered why it's so hard to swat a fly and why they always get away? It's because flies have huge eyes that see lots of little differences in time so they can move ten times as quickly as us. You'll see some funny things in this film: it has been slowed down to show how the people look to a fly and the tea looks like treacle! It also shows how slow the fly looks to the bird and how easy the catch is! The body of a dead shrew is rotting but this time the film is speeded up. And what about that fast-moving elephant? That's how quickly it would seem to go if it was small!

Q: Why did the children throw a clock out of the window?
A: *They wanted to see if time flies!*

Mix and match

To read out or act

'For everything there is a season and a time for every matter under heaven: a time to be born and a time to die . . .'
(Ecclesiastes 3 : 18)

A series of pairs of actions – apparently opposite in meaning yet paradoxically complementary – suggests a wide range of ways in which people use time. Reading this biblical passage will be all the more vivid if mimed by children or visualised through their art. The children might also question some of the actions, or add other paradox-pairs of actions from their own experience. 'There is a time for everything!' might be displayed as a banner and recited to draw the ideas together.

To read out

This classical myth has frightening aspects and implications for saying 'No!' to strangers. Exploring the meaning of time and presenting certain moral dilemmas, it has much to discuss, is not ruined by intervention – 'Should Demeter have neglected the earth? How could Zeus help?' – and lends itself to drama. If you can't get a pomegranate and open it to show the seeds, describe what it's like inside: it's fun to model!

Do you ever wonder why the seasons change? A long time ago, in Greece, people wondered that, and they told this story.

Persephone lived with her mother Demeter, who was also a mother to the earth: she watched over everything that grew and at harvest time she gathered it in. Every day was warm and bright: Persephone liked to talk with sea creatures, who made her beautiful necklaces of the best shells from their secret place under water. She wanted to give them a present, too, so she ran off to make them necklaces of pretty flowers. Just then, she noticed a bush covered in colourful, sweet-smelling blossoms and thought she would take it home for Demeter, but as she tugged at the bush, she heard a loud rumbling sound and a huge hole appeared! Out of it galloped four black horses, snorting red flames of fire, and pulling a chariot. A huge man leaned out and dragged Persephone in – imagine how frightened she was! He told her not to cry, that he was Pluto, the king of the underworld, who would take her down to his golden palace. It was lovely there and everybody was kind, but still Persephone missed her mother and wanted to go home. She became so sad that she could not eat. ●

All this time, Demeter was really worried and searched everywhere for Persephone but no one seemed to have seen her. Demeter stopped looking after the earth and soon everything started to die. After six months, there wasn't a single green spot on earth. Demeter was sad – and the whole world with her. But Zeus, the ruler of the world, assured her that Persephone was safe and that he would tell Pluto that she could come back if she hadn't eaten anything in the underworld.

Pluto had been worried that Persephone wasn't eating so he sent his servants up to get something she might like. The only thing growing was a pomegranate! It was the first food she had seen from her own world and she took a big bite! Then Pluto told her that she was free to go home! ▲

When Demeter saw Persephone, she smiled and tiny flowers peeped out. Their tears of joy watered the ground and made shoots appear. As they walked, grass grew, cows grazed and bird song filled the air. Demeter plucked an apple for Persephone to eat but she said she had *just* eaten four pomegranate seeds. Demeter knew what that meant and a shiver ran down her spine!

Sadly, they went to Zeus. At first he said Persephone had to go back as she had eaten down below, but Demeter told him that if her child went away she would be so upset that nothing could ever grow again. Zeus could not break his agreement but he could not let the earth starve. So he decided Persephone would stay in the underworld for one month for each seed she had eaten – and the rest of the year she could live with Demeter.

In winter, when the earth was bare and cold, the ancient Greeks thought of Demeter missing Persephone and longing for her to come back. And when Persephone did return each spring, Demeter was so happy that the earth turned green again with new life.

To read out

A boy called Christopher Robin imagines lots of stories about his toy animals. Pooh, his favourite, often gets in a muddle but really enjoys life – especially eating! – and he feels sorry for Eeyore, a sad and lonely donkey. Piglet is a bit nervous and always goes around with Pooh. Kanga helps and looks after other animals. Rabbit is serious, fussy and a bit of a busybody! He doesn't realise that any time can be *made* special.

'What *I* think,' said Pooh, 'is I think we'll go to Pooh Corner and see Eeyore, because perhaps his house has been blown down, and perhaps he'd like us to build it again.'

'What *I* think,' said Piglet, 'is I think we'll go and see Christopher Robin, only he won't be there, so we can't.'

'Let's go and see *everybody*,' said Pooh. 'Because when you've been walking in the wind for miles, and you suddenly go into somebody's house, and he says, "Hallo, Pooh, you're just in time for a little smackerel of something," and you are, then it's what I call a Friendly Day.' ●

Piglet thought they ought to have a Reason for going to see everybody . . . if Pooh could think of something. Pooh could.

'We'll go because it's Thursday,' he said, 'and we'll go to wish everybody a Very Happy Thursday. Come on, Piglet.'

They got up; and when Piglet had sat down again, because he didn't know the wind was so strong, and had been helped up by Pooh, they started off. They went to Pooh's house first, and luckily Pooh was at home just as they got there, so he asked them in, and they had some, and then they went on . . . By the time they got to Kanga's house they were so buffeted that they stayed to lunch. Just at first it seemed rather cold outside afterwards, so they pushed on to Rabbit's as quickly as they could. ▲

'We've come to wish you a Very Happy Thursday,' said Pooh . . .

'Why, what's going to happen on Thursday?' asked Rabbit, and when Pooh had explained, and Rabbit, whose life was made up of Important Things, said, 'Oh, I thought you'd really come about something,' they sat down for a little . . . and by-and-by Pooh and Piglet went on again . . .

'Rabbit's clever,' said Pooh thoughtfully.

'Yes,' said Piglet. 'Rabbit's clever.'

'And he has Brain.'

'Yes,' said Piglet, 'Rabbit has Brain.'

There was a long silence.

'I suppose,' said Pooh, 'that's why he never understands anything.'

(A. A. Milne, *The World of Pooh*, Methuen, 1928/58, pp. 272–4)

Book box

David McKee, *Not Now, Bernard*, Beaver, 1988, 0 09 924050 5. A popular and outrageously illustrated book on the run-along-and-don't-bother-me-now theme.

Peter Bonnici, *The Festival*, Mantra, 1984, 1 852690 631. In several dual-language versions and delicately illustrated, this tells of a Hindu boy's wonder at the preparations his family are making for the festival of the village temple.

Leo Lionni, 'Frederick', in *Frederick's Tales*, Andersen Press, 1986, 0 86264 140 3. A story about the harvest of time and human resources.

Mem Fox, *Wilfrid Gordon McDonald Partridge*, Kane/Miller, 1989, 0 916291 26 X. Hearing that old Miss Nancy has 'lost her memory', Wilfrid asks what memory means.

Valerie Flournoy, *The Patchwork Quilt*, Puffin, 1985, 0 14 050641 1. A poignant story of a Black girl and her Grandma who tenderly teaches her to find real beauty in things that take time.

Fiona French, *The Magic Vase*, Oxford University Press, 1990, 0 19 279875 8. A dramatically illustrated book about what really lasts . . .

The song

Happy Times Today!

This song, composed by Ester Gluck (aged 8), was transcribed by Walter Robson.

The lyrics are based on the Cantonese greeting for Chinese New Year but, for different times, other phrases may be substituted:

For the Hindu festival of Diwali: 'Shub Diwali' which means 'Happy Festival of Light!' The 'shub' sound is as in 'put' and 'diwali' is pronounced 'dee-wah-lee'.

For the Muslim festival of Eid-ul-Fitr which breaks the fast of Ramadan: 'Eid Mubarak' meaning 'Blessed Festival' and pronounced 'eed moo-bar-ak'.

For Jewish New Year: 'Shana Tova' which means 'Good Year!' and is pronounced 'shah-nah toh-vah'.

For Sikhs at any time: 'Sat sri akal' meaning 'God is truth'.

It also works for 'Happy Birthday' and 'Merry Christmas'!

Happily

Kung hey fat choy! Fun is here! Hap-py times to-day!
Love, peace and joy to all the world! Kung hey fat choy! Kung hey fat choy!

Closing thoughts

When birthdays are celebrated, one of these prayers, adapted to suit the child and the school, may be helpful:

I have lived another year and so have millions of other children born on the same day. I wonder what they are thinking now! I hope we will have a happy day and a happy year!

'Dear Father,
Today I am six and my gran says she is sixty.
I know that you love us both the same, though, Lord.
Thank you.'

(Carol Watson, *365 Children's Prayers*, Lion, 1990, 0 7324 0010 4, pp. 143, 336)

This meditation on the use of time lends itself to three readers; its form may be adapted as a prayer. . . .

'Our lives are made up of tiny moments and each one is important. We can spend each moment doing good or doing bad.

If we waste our hours, spoil our days and throw away our weeks, our lives will be empty. But if we see each hour as a chance, if we spend each day in growing and if we use each week to move ahead, our lives will be full.

And if we help one another to take each moment as a time to do good, our *whole* lives will be important to ourselves . . . to other people . . . and to God.'

1938 M. C. ESCHER/CORDON ART–BAARN–HOLLAND

20 I wonder ■ ■ ■

There is so much in life that we cannot explain or do not want to. Ironically, children need concrete ways of exploring the abstract and may respect God most through humour.

awe and mystery

Many adults understandably shrink from exploring with children ideas of ultimate reality, of the divine. Yet children themselves are receptive to that which is intangible or incomprehensible; and awe, mystery and wonder are part of their world. A wide range of sources, approached flexibly in an open atmosphere, can stimulate discovery and realisation, while securing protection from exposure or embarrassment.

Our dream-life is mysterious, intimate and precious: reflecting upon dreams is an important way in which children can 'name' their inner world and appreciate that all people – and perhaps animals too – hold within them something which is uniquely theirs. It may be tempting to invite children to recount their dreams – and they are likely to be eager to do so – but such discussions are difficult to manage productively and sensitively, and may be quite intrusive. Yet it is fulfilling to allow children to reflect silently – alone together, as it were – on dreams they remember; and such an atmosphere can validate a sense of awe about themselves.

Book box

Quite a lot of contemporary children's fiction deals with the power of the mind to create reality and with the parallels or tensions between the inner and outer world. Those noted below have had great impact on children, and reading any or all of them would be a 'stilling' close or follow-up to the exploration of dreams.

Hazel Edwards, *There's a Hippopotamus on our Roof Eating Cake*, Hodder and Stoughton, 1984, 0 340 28697 0. Especially delightful for the early years, this story lays the foundation for many concepts of God.

Kathleen Hersom, *Maybe It's a Tiger*, Macmillan, 1987, 0 333 32382 3. An all-too-rare book featuring a black child in the inner city.

Jack Kent, *There's No Such Thing as a Dragon*, Blackie, 1986, 0 216 91712 3. This story concerns a little boy's dragon who grows bigger every time adults deny its existence!

Anthony Browne, *Gorilla*, Magnet, 1988, 0 416 52460 5. Because of the subtlety and poignancy of the illustrations, they need to be seen at close range.

Raymond Briggs, *The Snowman Story Book*, Hamish Hamilton, 1990, 0 241 130 45X. After the picture book, the video and 'word' versions by others, the author has created a text to accompany his original pictures, making this book suitable for reading aloud.

Barbara Resch, *The Elephant with Rosy-Coloured Ears*, A. and C. Black, 1979, 0 7136 1392 0. Big Elephant is ashamed of his pink ears, but the Baby Elephant says they cheer the place up!

Anthony Browne, *Look What I've Got!*, Magnet, 1987, 0 416 95940 7. The experiences here will resonate more with Junior children and the delicate illustrations beg to be examined closely.

Leo Lionni, 'Geraldine, the Music Mouse', in *Frederick's Tales*, Andersen Press, 1986, 0 86264 140 3. The bold 'naïve' illustrations are a delight to hold up; this story is best appreciated by older children.

To read out

There is much to explore and examine in the following pupil's story and it lends itself to mime and other forms of dramatisation. If it follows a period of personal thought, it can be satisfying and effective.

Did you have a dream last night? Of course you did! We all dream when we sleep but we don't always remember it. Think about a dream you once had: is it easy to understand what's going on, or is everything a bit mixed up? Some people think that their dreams tell them something very important about themselves, or bring them messages from someone who died, or make them feel that God is near. Ivan El-Minyawa (age 11) wondered why we dream, where the ideas in our dreams come from and why our dreams don't seem to mean anything. He wrote this story:

Once, long ago, when the world was still young, it was ruled by the powerful Calamor. At that time, the world was perfect except for one thing: only Calamor had dreams since that was his link with the gods. Because the people had no dreams, when they fell asleep, the world was dark. This made them afraid to sleep and because they did not sleep, they were too tired to do any work, such as giving sacrifices.

So Calamor prayed to the gods and they gave people dreams – but not ordinary dreams. In these dreams, the gods spoke to them so that they knew what to do the next day. ●

One night when Calamor was in bed, he thought, 'Now the people can hear the gods' wishes for themselves, maybe they won't need me to tell them ... and then I won't be the ruler any more!' So all that night, he made a spell and, when at last the morning came, he cast it. The spell made the people have dreams which were meaningless.

Then the gods found out! But they could not change the spell because it was so powerful. So they took their revenge by killing Calamor with a lightning bolt.

Mix and match

An activity

An important element in introducing the awesome nature of God is the concept of infinity. This can be visualised through a Mobius strip: you will need a strip of paper about 60 cm by 10 cm in size (it's more vivid if each side is a different colour). Give it a half-twist and stick the two ends together. Then, using a bold-coloured pen, start in the middle of the width and draw a line along the length of the strip. You will see that the paper now has only one side and that your pen comes back to where it started! Cut along the line and you should have made a figure-of-eight! With practice, you could demonstrate a small version to the children before their very eyes or a group of pupils could have made a huge one in advance and perform show-and-tell, displaying the various stages in the style of 'Here's one we made earlier!' This is a simple but effective way in which children of all ages can comprehend the notion of 'going on for ever'.

To read out or act

This story lends itself to mime: it is fun to have a group perform it without introduction and to allow the others to suggest its meaning!

When Guru Nanak, the first Sikh guru, was in Mecca, the centre of the Islamic world, he was criticised for showing disrespect by sitting with his feet pointing towards the Ka'aba, since it is the focal point of Muslim prayers. Guru Nanak replied that God was everywhere and he challenged his critics to point his feet in any direction where God was not!

When telling this story – or having children enact it – it may be wise not to mention the Islamic context as it risks showing Muslims in a bad light: it is potentially distressing for Muslim pupils and might encourage negative attitudes in non-Muslims. The well-loved Sikh story intends no specifically anti-Muslim polemic and loses none of its impact if it is simply stated that Guru Nanak went somewhere where people had a special place . . .

The video

Psalm 139 (creatively treated in clip number 20 on the accompanying video cassette) is found in the Bible and used by Jews and Christians. The clip uses split-screen effects and a short but evocative piece of film of a baby in the womb. It may be helpful to read the Psalm before or after showing the video, and as a basis for expressing some of the images in art.

A man drives into a council estate, gets out of his car and starts running up and down the steps, along the corridors, in and out of the doors and he crashes into the fencing . . . At first, he seems to be running away from something or somebody. In his mind, a poem says that he cannot get away from God, that God knows everything about him and has thoughts that he could never understand: God could see him before he was born, when he was still inside his mother's tummy where it is dark. But darkness isn't dark for God because God is nothing like anything or anyone else. In the end, the man stops wanting to get away from God and stops wanting God to get away from him. He asks God to stay and be with him.

Book box

Etan Boritzer, *What is God?*, Firefly, 1990, 0 920668 88 7. An unusual book, vividly illustrated, and written as though talking to children about the feelings they may have about God.

Tomie de Paola, *The Clown of God*, Methuen, 1985, 0 416 61710 7. A traditional tale, retold and boldly illustrated, on the theme of life itself as divine service and prayer as power. Children will need some introduction to monasticism and to the elevation of the Blessed Virgin Mary in Catholic worship.

20

To read out

The idea of formal prayer might best be introduced to children by looking at other children's experiences. Sometimes pupils will spontaneously make up prayers in the context of reflecting on what they are learning and they may be willing to share these with others; yet frequently the prevailing 'pop culture' or 'macho ethos' militates against this, leaving an individual vulnerable to ridicule. This extract deals with many of the issues children themselves face and lends itself neatly to a dialogue between a female teacher and a girl, with a narrator.

Anne Shirley is an imaginative and chatty orphan who has red hair which she hates. She grew up in a children's home but is adopted by an elderly sister and brother, Marilla and Matthew Cuthbert, who are kind but very set in their ways and not used to children. Soon after Anne arrives at Green Gables, Marilla comes to her room at bed-time and tells her to say her prayers.

'I never say any prayers,' announced Anne.

Marilla looked with horrified astonishment. 'Why, Anne, what do you mean? Were you never taught to say your prayers? God always wants little girls to say their prayers . . . I'm afraid you are a very bad little girl.'

'You'd find it easier to be bad than good if you had red hair,' said Anne reproachfully. 'People who haven't red hair don't know what trouble is. Mrs Thomas told me God made my hair red *on purpose*, and I've never cared about Him since. And anyhow, I'd always be too tired at night to bother saying prayers . . .' ●

'You must say your prayers while you're under my roof, Anne.'

'Why, of course, if you want me to . . . But you'll have to tell me what to say for this once. After I get into bed I'll imagine out a real nice prayer to say always. I believe that it will be quite interesting, now that I come to think of it.'

'You must kneel down,' said Marilla in embarrassment . . .

'Why must people kneel down to pray? If I really wanted to pray, I'll tell you what I'd do. I'd go out into a great big field all alone or into the deep, ▶

185

deep woods, and I'd look up into the sky – up – up – up – into that lovely blue sky that looks as if there was no end to its blueness. And then I'd just *feel* a prayer. Well, I'm ready. What am I to say?' ▲

'You're old enough to pray for yourself, Anne,' said Marilla. 'Just thank God for your blessings and ask Him humbly for the things you want.'

'Well, I'll do my best,' promised Anne, burying her face in Marilla's lap. 'Gracious heavenly Father . . . I thank Thee for . . . the Lake of Shining Waters and Bonny and the Snow Queen. I'm really extremely grateful for them. And that's all the blessings I can think of just now to thank Thee for. As for the things I want, they're so numerous that it would take a great deal of time to name them all, so I will only mention the two most important. Please let me stay at Green Gables; and please let me be good-looking when I grow up. I remain,
Yours respectfully,
ANNE SHIRLEY.'

(L. M. Montgomery, *Anne of Green Gables*, Puffin, 1908/1977, 0 14 032 462 3, pp. 46–8)

To read out

The concept of uniqueness is a significant element in children's awareness of God. This extract is difficult for children to read aloud, paradoxically because of the child-like language – and the spelling is not to be emulated!

Anna is a girl who has a friend called Fin. She wonders about many things and thinks God is not like anyone or anything else.

Mister God is like a pensil . . . but a pensil you can not see, so you not see what shape it is, but can draw all the shapes ther is and this is like Mister God. When you grow up you get a bit funy becase you want Mister God to have a propre shape like an old man and wiskers and wrinkels on his face but Mister God do not look like that . . .

How can you say of Mister God . . . But I can becase I have a sekrit book Fin give to me. It is a pictur book all about snow flak and every snowflak is not the same. If you look at a snowflak shape it is not the same as another snowflak shape, so it has not got a propre snowflak shape. But you can only call it snow and you can not call it a shape and you see THAT IS LIKE MISTER GOD. You can not call Mister God a thing and you can not call Mister God a shape and you can only call Mister God Mister God.

(Fynn, *Anna's Book*, Collins, 1986, 0 00 627119 7, pp. 21f)

To read out

Nine-year-old children from Salusbury Junior School were invited to express their idea of God. It is often 'safer' to read to pupils the writings of children they do not know:

'I love God because he is our God and he made us and the ladybird and the beetle and Ms J. Brown and my friends. God loves us and we should be good to God.'
(Stella Ramsay)

'I believe in God because he makes your arms, legs, brain, ears and nose. He even makes the whole world. No one can stop me loving God. He even tries to stop people dying but no one knows. I think when the sun comes out, he is happy. When the rain comes down, he's sad. I wish I could see God. He must be beautiful and loving. Sometimes I pray and sometimes I forget.'
(Tamika Davis)

'I think God looks like a spirit. He also has magical powers and can heal people. I think he lives in a mansion in heaven with lots of angels as servants and carol singers as butlers. In his garden grow bread, wine, apples, Ribena, strawberries and raspberries.'
(Katherine Gordon)

'God is the biggest in the world. I like God very much and I like things which God gives us. God never sleeps. God just looks at what's happening. God helps those who pray. Nobody can have God's place.'
(Alia Saleem)

'God is in the trees.

God is in the breeze.

God is here, there and everywhere.

Heaven is the place to be

because it's there you can be free.

God can be a he or she.

God is proud.

God is a cloud.

God can be anything.'

(Glenn Cresswell)

To read out

It is a tenet of the Empiricist school of philosophy that only that which can be experienced can be said to exist: a popular but anonymous limerick was generated to express this standpoint. An equally anonymous limerick soon emerged on the theme that everything exists because God is, as it were, the universal 'experiencer'. This is a modern, child-oriented version!

An activity

Philosophers (including many children!) sometimes wrestle with the idea of whether something can exist without anybody to experience it. Tell the children that when we hear something it is because sound waves have reached our eardrums. Then ask them if a tree fell in a forest and there were no people or animals in the forest, whether the tree would make a sound.

There once was a child who said, 'God

Must wonder why it's so odd

When he sees that this pea

Can still manage to be,

When no one can get in its pod!'

Dear Child, you're quite funny and odd!

I can get in the *tiniest* pod!

And that's why the pea

Will continue to be

As it's seen by me, all-seeing God!

To read out or act

This 'old chestnut' originally involved an ink-well, now a cup is more appropriate. Do the actions as you tell the joke or, better still, prime a child to play the part of the pupil.

A teacher was once telling her class that God was everywhere but the children couldn't see how that could be. One of them asked, 'Do you mean God's here in this classroom?'

'Certainly!' said the teacher.

'Is God in this cup, then?' replied the child.

'Oh yes!' answered the teacher. 'Even in this cup!'

Slamming a hand over the top of the cup, the child exclaimed, 'Got him!'

Closing thoughts

Staff and pupils of Oaklands Special School, Hounslow, created this prayer: around the hall are pupils' pictures, each depicting, in order, the meaning of a line. Those who do not know the prayer by heart can 'read' the pictures on the walls.

God is in the mountain.
God is in the sea.
God is in the rainbow.
God is in the trees.
God is in the sunshine.
God is in the rain.
God is in the flowers.
Please God, be in me.

'Teach me, my God and King,
In all things Thee to see,
That what I do in anything
To do it unto Thee.'

(George Herbert, Anglican; 1593–1632)

Index of Religions and Cultures

Aborigine, 14
African, 14, 19, 27, 31, 39, 41, 75, 87, 96, 104, 106, 107, 127, 151
Amerindian, 14, 27, 49, 92, 104, 163
Australian, 14, 19, 52, 83

Baha'i, 25
Bedouin, 40
Bengali, 41, 145
Black, 26, 73, 106, 140, 148, 151–3, 178, 182
Buddhist, 22, 46, 53, 163

Caribbean, 44, 67, 72–3
Chinese, 12, 19, 22, 34, 35, 67, 106, 134–5, 156, 160, 168, 179
Christian, 19, 26, 32, 35, 38, 41, 54, 56, 60, 67, 75, 83, 104, 107, 117, 127, 134, 135, 139, 145, 171, 174–5, 179, 184, 185–6, 189
Cuban, 62
Czech, 35

Filipino, 22, 141
Finnish, 63
French, 32, 72, 114–15

German, 102
Greek, 175–6
Gujarati, 167

Hindu, 27, 31–3, 41, 49, 56, 62, 107, 178, 179

Indian, 24, 31, 35, 49, 57, 62, 122
Inuit, 62, 71, 80, 104
Irish, 27, 111

Jain, 122–3
Japanese, 127, 171
Jewish, 32, 33, 45, 46, 48, 57, 64, 66, 75, 90, 96, 106, 126, 130, 151, 160, 174–5, 179, 184

Maori, 83, 111
Middle Eastern, 74, 168

Muslim, 26, 40, 56, 57, 73, 74, 85, 94–5, 171, 179, 184
North American, 67, 80, 83, 92, 114, 166
Punjabi, 150

Rastafarian, 62, 107
Romany, 143–5
Russian, 80, 168

Sikh, 49, 75, 90–1, 116–17, 171, 179, 184
South American, 52, 83, 97
Spanish, 97

Welsh, 16, 104, 132

Index of Subjects

Animals, 14, 15–16, 24, 26, 27, 31, 38, 39, 40, 45, 52, 56, 75, 80, 81–2, 83, 100–2, 104, 106, 122, 127, 132–3, 138, 140, 142–3, 145, 161, 162–3, 166, 168, 171, 174, 182

Babies, 11, 93, 151, 171
Birds and eggs, 12, 13, 14, 15, 16, 18, 23, 24, 27, 31, 38, 46, 52, 53, 56, 101, 106, 107, 114–15, 120–1, 127, 134–5, 138, 141, 142, 160, 163, 168, 171, 174
Bodies, 14, 16–18, 83, 165–71
Books and writings, 26, 46, 70, 90, 92, 93, 96, 106, 107, 124–5, 156–8, 184, 186

Children, 16–17, 24, 32–3, 35, 38, 39, 41, 49, 53, 62, 73, 75, 76–7, 83, 84, 87, 89, 91, 93, 106, 110, 111, 114–15, 124–5, 127, 132–4, 137–9, 140, 143–5, 148, 151–3, 158–9, 160, 163, 166, 171, 175–6, 178, 179, 185–6, 189
Clothes and fabrics, 26, 27, 32, 34, 46, 56, 57, 60, 63, 83, 106, 111, 115, 132, 135, 144, 149, 160, 163, 169, 178

Colours, 16–17, 30–1, 32–3, 35, 44, 46–7, 66, 74, 83, 97, 114, 117, 135, 171, 175–6, 182

Communities, 60, 62, 79–87, 102–3, 104–7, 116–17, 139, 143–5. 153, 156, 168, 175–6

Creation, 11–19, 38, 39, 45–7, 49, 53–5, 57, 72–4, 83, 104–5, 106, 111, 163, 166, 175–7, 187

Dance and movement, 12–13, 24, 32–3, 44, 46, 66, 82, 84, 87, 92, 106, 127, 130, 151–3, 156–7, 171, 184–5

Death, 13, 15, 17, 18, 57, 60, 61, 63, 96, 97, 106, 113, 116–17, 122, 156

Disability and illness, 22–3, 32, 61, 63, 117, 124–5, 135

Dolls and toys, 35, 53, 132, 168, 169–70, 177–8

Earth, 14, 15, 23, 25, 27, 39, 44, 46–7, 49, 52–5, 57, 87, 94–5, 104, 138, 161, 163, 175–6

Eating and drinking, 32, 60, 61, 63, 65, 69–77, 83, 84, 90, 91, 94–5, 97, 100–2, 107, 112, 114, 132, 134, 151–3, 166, 169, 171, 176, 187

Elderly, 57, 84, 171, 178, 179, 185

Families, 45, 46, 49, 60, 66, 75, 83, 84, 92, 96, 102, 106, 107, 112, 114, 116, 122–3, 132, 140, 143–5, 151–3, 163, 166, 171, 175–6, 178, 179

Feelings, 24, 26, 35, 60, 61, 62, 66, 67, 92, 93, 97, 103, 106, 121, 124–5, 130, 132, 133–4, 137–45, 147–53, 156–7, 163, 184

Festivals and seasons, 24, 32, 33, 34, 60, 72, 75, 134, 135, 173–9

Fire, 30–1, 49, 104, 132, 143–5

Fish, 38, 71, 112–13, 120, 160, 161, 168

Flowers, 19, 47, 52, 66, 96, 117, 138, 142, 161–3, 167, 175, 176, 189

Friends, 32–3, 39, 62, 63, 66, 67, 80, 84, 91, 100, 102, 107, 112, 149, 177–8

Fruit, 49, 52, 57, 74, 86, 175, 176

Games and sport, 24, 82, 110–11, 120–1, 127, 130, 132, 139–40, 145

Gifts, 24, 40, 60, 67, 75, 135

God, 13, 14, 19, 23, 27, 32, 39, 41, 44, 45, 46–7, 49, 52, 56, 57, 59, 62, 66, 67, 72, 74, 83, 85, 97, 104–5, 106, 107, 116, 117, 120, 133–4, 135, 139, 140, 145, 148, 153, 160, 166, 176, 179, 182, 183, 184, 185, 186, 187, 188, 189

Governments, 52, 96, 102, 156, 157

Homes, 31, 49, 60, 61, 62, 63, 64, 66, 76, 77, 132, 143–5, 171, 175, 176, 185–6

Humour, 12, 13, 26, 33–4, 38, 40, 44, 45, 46–7, 53, 57, 63, 66, 70, 75, 77, 82, 83, 90, 91, 97, 100–2, 106, 111, 112–13, 127, 151–3, 160, 169, 174, 177–8, 185–6, 188, 189

Imaginary and prehistoric creatures, 38, 46, 114–15, 160, 182

Journeys and adventures, 21–7, 38, 90–1, 96, 102, 107, 112–13, 120–1, 132–3, 161–3

Love, 31, 59–67, 72, 82, 84, 96, 106, 107, 120, 132, 134, 139, 145, 187

Men and women, 15, 16, 17, 19, 39, 49, 59–67, 87, 96, 104, 151

Mountains and stones, 13, 14, 16, 25, 26, 27, 39, 57, 189

Music and sound, 23, 24, 32, 46, 49, 66, 67, 111, 117, 156, 171

Pain and sorrow, 17, 30, 56, 60, 61, 63, 72, 92, 93, 97, 107, 116, 132, 133, 137–45, 147–53

Peace and war, 22–3, 27, 31, 32, 56, 82, 83, 84, 96, 97, 107, 116

Places, 14, 15, 25, 26, 32, 46, 64, 96, 106, 175–6, 184

Religious buildings, 32, 56, 57, 64–5, 75, 90, 139, 153, 184

Religious figures, 25, 31, 32, 38, 41, 49, 56, 57, 67, 90–1, 96, 107, 116, 130, 134, 135, 139, 160, 184

School, 61, 75, 83, 110, 111, 124–5, 148, 156, 174

Seeds and harvest, 18, 19, 54–5, 57, 72–3, 122–3, 138, 175–6, 178

Shapes and sizes, 30–1, 77, 97, 148, 149, 158, 159, 160, 168, 182, 186, 187, 188

Sky, 13, 14, 16, 31, 57, 83, 163, 186

Trees, 13, 16, 23, 46, 49, 57, 83, 86, 106, 188, 189

Vehicles, 16, 19, 24, 31, 66, 92, 161, 175

Water, 14, 16, 22, 23, 24, 32, 37–41, 44, 49, 61, 66, 70, 72, 77, 80, 104, 114, 130, 134

Wealth and poverty, 40, 67, 96, 94, 114–15, 122–3

Weather, 41, 43–4, 94–5

Work, 16, 60, 92, 107, 114–15, 132

Acknowledgements

Working with teachers and children is always enriching and ennobling: I am humbled by their openness to possibilities for worship, stimulated by their encouragement to develop new approaches and deepened by all they have contributed to my own growth over several years.

There are many that I cannot name but I would especially like to record my thanks for the motivation of John Logan and all the teachers in the Hounslow 'Worship Collective'; the support of Bill Laar, Tim Feast, Linda Squire, Marjorie Broadhead, Malcolm Gifford and Tony Shield, fellow Inspectors in Westminster LEA; our professional partnership with David Barton of the London Diocesan Board for Schools; and the awesome inspiration of Maurice Lynch, Director of the BFSS National RE Centre.

Much of the raw material in *Assembly Kit* has never been published before. I am touched by the readiness of children to express their thoughts and feelings and particularly appreciate those at Salusbury Junior School (Brent) who gave of themselves so generously, and their teachers whose sensitivity elicited some very profound insights.

Music plays an important part in worship: the inherited songs willingly shared by Christine Chin, Kanta Gomez, Samira Habashi, Indira Sen and Kulwant Wassu lend both authenticity and diversity. Through worship, people not only reach deep into themselves but can also stretch across the world and down the ages: Stephen Clark's original compositions – songs based on traditional stories yet with a thoroughly contemporary feel – make that a creative and exciting possibility. It is through Walter Robson's rigorous musicianship and painstaking attention to detail, and Jack Thompson's careful engraving, that the printed music was produced – often from my very amateur recordings and scores!

Every single item in *Assembly Kit* has been scrutinised by children: their perceptive and critical minds helped to shape the selection, and their wisdom and empathy has informed the guidance that is offered for others. I am most of all grateful to Ester Gluck who so often acted as a guinea pig – though her own preference is for hamsters!

Picture credits

CHRIS ASKWITH front cover (sunflowers), BARNABY'S PICTURE LIBRARY pages 10 (Mark Boulton), 50 (Mustograph), 118 (John Rocha), 128 (C. M. Radcliffe) & 172 (H. Kanus); BRITISH MUSEUM page 154; COLIN BUTLER page 78; CAMERA PRESS page 108 (Hong Kong Government Information Service); © 1938 M. C. ESCHER/CORDON ART-BAARN-HOLLAND page 180; SALLY & RICHARD GREENHILL pages 58, 68 & 98; HONG KONG TOURIST ASSOCIATION page 28; MAGNUM pages 88 (Bruno Barbey) & 146 (Peter Marlow); REX FEATURES pages 20, 36 (Sipa-Press), 42 (A. Devaney) & 136 (George Konig). The picture on page 164 was taken for the BBC.

Acknowledgement is due to the following whose permission is required for multiple reproduction:

JUDY DAISH ASSOCIATES LTD for 'Boundaries Down' and 'Pan Gu' by Stephen Clark; SHELDON VIDIBOR INC. for 'I Won't Hatch', 'Hug O' War', 'No Difference', 'Alice' and 'Ma and God' by Shel Silverstein; 'Which Came First' from *Laughter is an Egg* published by Penguin 1990, 'Rainbow' from *Mangoes and Bullets* published by Pluto Press 1985 and 'I'd Like to Squeeze' from *You'll Love This Stuff* by kind permission of JOHN AGARD c/o Caroline Sheldon Literary Agency; KATHY GALLOWAY for the extract from the *Iona Community Worship Book* © 1988 The Iona Community/Wild Goose Publications, Glasgow, Scotland; CAROLYN ASKAR for 'Spirit of Fire' from *Spirit of Fire* published by Element Books Ltd 1983; DAVID HIGHAM ASSOCIATES for *Kamla and Kate* by Jamila Gavin; PETER CUNNINGHAM for the extract from *Fire Words* published by Jonathan Cape; EXLEY PUBLICATIONS LTD for 'Twinkle Twinkle Little Star' and 'Jack and Jill be Nimble' by Douglas Larche and for the extract by Paula Lagerstam from *Dear World*; CARL SANDBERG for the prologue to *The Family of Man* published by The Museum of Modern Art, New York; HAMISH HAMILTON LTD for the extract from *Charlotte's Web* by E.B. White; PAN BOOKS for the extracts from *Jonathan Livingston Seagull* by Richard Bach and *The Little Prince* by Antoine de Saint-Exupery; ANN HOLM for the extract from *I Am David* and A.A. MILNE for the extract from *The World of Pooh* published by Methuen Children's Books; VICTOR GOLLANCZ LTD for 'The Pudding Like A Night On The Sea' from *The Julian Stories* by Ann Cameron; HARPER COLLINS for the extract from *Anna's Book* by Fynn; PUFFIN BOOKS for the extract from *Anne of Green Gables* by L.M. Montgomery © Ruth and David MacDonald. All rights reserved; DELL BOOKS for the extract from *There's No Such Place As Far Away* by Richard Bach © 1979 by Richard Bach; PAN McMILLAN CHILDREN'S BOOKS for the extract from *The Diddakoi* by Rumer Godden; *A Fish of The World* by Terry Jones by permission of PAVILLION BOOKS; BLACKIE AND SON LTD for 'Exams' ed. by Louise Carpenter and the untitled prayer by Timothy King taken from *The Puffin Book of Prayers*; WALKER BOOKS LTD for 'Beneath the Surface' by Jonathan McKay and the extract from 'Through the Eyes of a Dyslexic' by Justin Hydes taken from *As I See It* © 1990 Dyslexia Institute; MARJERY WILLIAMS for the extract from *The Velveteen Rabbit* published by William Heinemann.

The Publishers have made every attempt to trace the copyright holders, but in cases where they may have failed will be pleased to make the necessary arrangements at the first opportunity.